POWER BEHIND YOUR WRITING

Kirk House Publishers

POWER BEHIND YOUR WRITING

What Every Writer Needs to Know

Evelyn D. Klein, M.S.T.

First Edition
Paperback ISBN: 978-1-959681-28-1
eBook ISBN: 978-1-959681-29-8
Hardcover ISBN: 978-1-959681-30-4
Library of Congress Control Number: 2023923297

Cover and Interior Design by Ann Aubitz based on a drawing by Evelyn D. Klein

Cover art and book illustrations by Evelyn D. Klein.

Published by Kirk House Publishers
1250 E 115th Street
Burnsville, MN 55337
Kirkhousepublishers.com
612-781-2815

ACKNOWLEDGMENTS

It is with much appreciation that the author acknowledges the support of her colleagues in the field of secondary education who encouraged this much needed project. Ultimately, this effort led to expansion of the original material for inclusion of a more wide-spread user base, pointing the way to publication of this book.

Great appreciation goes out to Lorraine Palkert Ph.D. and Rhonda Petree M.A., ESL for their time and consideration in reviewing *Power Behind Your Writing.*

Many thanks go to Michael Woolsey, board member of the Minnesota Independent Scholars Forum, for his faith in and support of this project.

For their support and inspiration, the author acknowledges her daughter, Angie and her son, Bill, who, also, helped with technological challenges.

This book is dedicated to the memory of my mother, Henrietta Klein, who first taught me the value of language and the importance of good writing, and to the students, young and adult, who inspire me.

INTRODUCTION

Not so long ago, the question "What pronouns do you prefer?" would not have made sense to most people, but now it is a common introductory question in many settings. It is only because of the recent global pandemic that the terms *social distancing* and *super-spreader event* became common in everyday English. While it is interesting to consider current additions and changes to the English language, these are not new phenomena. The English language is always in flux due to changes in society, influences from other languages, and emerging communication trends. In the new book, *Power Behind Your Writing: What Every Writer Needs to Know*, Evelyn Klein explains that being informed about the historical changes of the English language, as well as its structural components will help students be more effective and successful writers.

Power Behind Your Writing: What Every Writer Needs to Know is composed of two parts. The first, "Our Changing Language," contains two sections – "Roots and Branches" and "The Story of English." In the first section, Klein explains how language is acquired and how English evolved along with other Indo-European languages. A chapter on cognates makes the relationship between these languages clear. In "The Story of English," Klein offers a concise and readable history of Old, Middle, and Modern English. This section is filled with examples of how words entered the English language through contact with different peoples and how the certain words can be traced through the times. The chapters end with questions to further the readers' thinking.

For people looking for an easy-to-use, helpful reference source, the second part of the book titled, "Components, Structures and Principles of Language" will be valuable. Each chapter in the first section, "Sentence Components: Parts of Speech" begins with a short, engaging poem, then provides clear definitions and explanations of the different parts of speech along with relevant examples, and ends with a segment called "Exploring Language" that offers creative application activities. These activities ask readers to identify the part of speech in the poem at the beginning of the chapter, complete short writing tasks using the part of speech and other noticing tasks. While these activities are optional, they provide an immediate application opportunity for those engaged with the chapter. In the second section titled, "Language Structures that Carry Writing: Sentence Types," Klein emphasizes the importance of clear and meaningful communication by way of well-constructed sentences. As in the previous section, these chapters end with a segment titled, "Exploring Writing" which asks the reader to apply the information into one's own writing or to notice how sentence types are used in authentic written communication.

Teachers and students alike will find this book useful. Teachers can access and reference specific sections as they prepare their own units and lessons. Teachers could also assign specific chapters to students for background reading on the developments of the English language or for information on parts of speech or types of sentences. Students who want or need a concise history of the English language for research or writing projects will find the first part of the book informative and accessible. The second part will be particularly useful to writing students when they are uncertain about how to use particular words or how to construct different types of sentences. The information is readable, and the explanations and examples are clear. Both native and non-native English speakers will find value in this book. Teachers and students alike will benefit from the chapter titled, "Punctuation Revisited" as it offers concise, useful information about correct punctuation usage.

Power Behind Your Writing: What Every Writer Needs to Know is a highly readable book and an easy-to-use reference tool. The text moves quickly through topics allowing the reader to take in a lot of information from each page. Intricate detailed illustrations at the beginning of some chapters further enhance the reader's experience with the content. The English language will continue to change to reflect the needs of modern society. With this book, teachers and students will be well-equipped to write effectively in our ever-changing world.

~Rhonda Petree
M.A. English as a Second Language
Secondary Teacher Certification
Fulbright Scholar, Estonia, 2028-2019
Lecturer, Department of English, TESOL, and Modern Languages
University of Wisconsin, River Falls
March 2022

CONTENTS

FROM NEED TO PURPOSE

Reference Book or Text

Power Behind Your Writing: What Every Writer Needs to Know is intended for the digital generation. It offers an updated, user-friendly look at the intricacies of the English language whether in speech or writing. Writers of varying backgrounds and fields, from college student to adult, from academic to technologist, journalist to creative writer among them will find it a convenient resource, not only for dealing with common writing problems but for shedding light on what appear to be inconsistencies of the English language. Grammar and language usage have been presented in their relevancy to writing in a new, easy-to-understand, accessible format, rich in examples. The book can serve both as textbook or reference source for writers in general, as guide for second language learners, and home-bound instruction.

Since our ability to use language reflects not only who we are as individuals in a diverse society but the region and age in which we live, it is helpful to be aware that language is constantly in flux, affecting or changing usage, denotation and connotation of words, and use of grammar which, in turn, affect how well and effectively we communicate with others.

Most of the material in this book is the outcome of content written for and taught in the classroom for several years, intended to give writers a better understanding of language basics, structure, and changes. This is accomplished in ways that rely on dependable patterns and coherence within English with relevancy to today's language usage, without being tedious.

The sequence of parts and chapters of the book has been carefully planned in a deliberate and systematic yet easy-to-follow approach for connection, continuity, and clarity. Part I of the book, Our Changing Language, is a brief illumination of origins and developments of the English language, permitting readers and students to see how language developed as part of the Indo-European language family, demystifying its seeming inconsistencies. Part II, Sentence Components, Structures and Principles of Language, Section A offers a well-rounded look, at Sentence Components: Parts of Speech. Their identification and function in the sentence are illuminated, applying a combination of traditional and functional grammar for easy understanding and consistency. Section B, Language Structures that Carry Writing: Sentence Types, explains construction and use of various sentence types. At the same time, use and function of punctuation is clarified. Each chapter in Part II is introduced with a brief creative writing selection to stimulate interest and to highlight and connect writing with grammar and sentence structure. Each chapter ends with a summary and suggestions for writing exercises.

Perspective

As effective and accurate language is waning in classroom and adult world, media or business, conversation and writing, some questions bear asking: Why did we first lose the connection between basic language skills and effective communication? Did people go off on a tangent teaching grammar for its own sake, without showing the relationship to appropriate speaking or writing? Did they make the subject too cumbersome? Then, there are those who are quick to point out: "Everybody else talks that way [with grammatical errors]. Why not me?" While conversation or spontaneous speaking allows us considerable leeway, writing or formal speaking call greater attention to grammatical errors, inconsistencies, or inaccuracies of meaning.

Or were people so intrigued with the discovery of the creative writing process in the 1970s and 1980s that they decided all we need is to write down our ideas, thinking of grammar, mechanics, or word choice as incidental? More recently, the effects of technology on language usage are also clearly evident.

From the time students enter school, they are encouraged to write from their own experience, be creative, imaginative, and original. And that is good. Yet once ideas are recorded, it is time to look at the mechanics of writing as well as updated usage of words and expressions. As writers mature, demands on writing often become increasingly complex. When writers have difficulty composing effective sentences, they can easily lapse into a conundrum or arrive at a brick wall of frustration attempting to write anything from business letters to reports, essays and articles to research papers, from poetry to stories and books, to say nothing of technical writing.

And, of course, our choice of words has a significant bearing on how our message is received, not only for the ordinary words but also for those words that carry social, racial, or sexual context. Their use and meaning may change not only over centuries but also in the present. This kind of language updating can seek many spontaneous classroom situations.

Reference Book

Over the years I have frequently helped out with writing problems as friend and community member. But as teacher in the public schools and later as writing instructor at a community college on the adult level, I have seen writing skills improve quickly using materials from this book. The waning away of writing skills in general, beginning with the student population moved to many working adults, including many professionals. Not surprisingly, at a recent publishers conference in the Midwest, publishers lamented the lack of writing quality of increasing numbers of books that make it into print. Most conspicuously, newspaper articles are increasingly dotted with grammatical errors. User's manuals are quickly becoming extinct for lack of those capable of writing specific, consistent, and accurate directions for product use. The use of e-mails and texting, frequently with their abbreviated, condensed style has added to the problem and misconception that accurate use of language is of little importance.

It became clear to me and my colleagues that a stronger background of language skills was needed for successful writing. Subsequently, I developed a quick crash course in grammar, serving as introductory material to writing, which eventually became *Power Behind Your Writing: What Every Writer Needs to Know*, Part II. Once students understood the role of grammar in constructing effective sentences, their writing took off.

Similarly, in world languages classes, students did not know how their own English language worked. Thus, they had trouble learning the second language under consideration. Consequently, the lesson would have to involve two parts, first the English version of grammar, then the foreign language. Again, here was inspiration for the book.

Yet another background was still missing, since language is intricately interwoven with cultural and historical developments. This was a topic I included in a linguistics class and with great success. It became Part I, Our Changing Language. It envisions how humans first acquire language, the development of English as part of the Indo-European family of languages and how historical developments, discoveries, inventions, social change, diversity, and gender issues contributed and continue, increasingly, to affect vocabulary and how we see the world. This gave students a larger perspective of their language and its on-going, often dynamic changes.

Not surprisingly, employers stress the need for employees to have at least a basic knowledge of good writing skills, even in the face of technology. And the military requires enlistees to have a basic command of language to read and understand written information and instructions in the manuals. Technology, despite its obvious conveniences, capabilities, and purposes is, at times, a run-away horse, both in its accessibility and language use. Needless to say, good writing skills are indispensable for the successful practice of business, development of ideas, recording and explanation of technical and scientific findings, research, technological practice and process, in creative writing, and on. Consequently, many of the larger employers have established their own education departments to manage the growing problem. Similarly, many colleges have remedial English programs for entering freshmen.

For the above reasons, my teaching colleagues and other writers encouraged completion of this timely book. It aims to fill a void by helping interested individuals and writers understand better how language works, so they can ultimately focus on the what and less on the how of their writing. After all, language provides the wings that take us anywhere we choose to go. Grammar supplies the structure that carries us and allows us to share the journey.

For a writer, whether college student preparing a research paper, employee putting together a report or user's manual, academic penning research findings, or professional writer opting for effect, language is the most important tool in establishing meaning, communication, effect, and credibility. For what we say can be as important as how we say it. With its updated, tested approach, richness of examples, and easy-to-follow format, *Power Behind Your Writing: What Every Writer Needs to Know,* dealing with the essentials of the English language, seeks to meet these needs. Once we see how all the pieces fit together, we can make sense of the whole. The book is also based on the premise that today's students and writers want to know why they need to learn something. This book allows them to study it in its entirety or take away only those aspects needed for occasional reference. It serves as an important resource and reference and is as indispensable as a good dictionary.

I. Our Changing Language

Words are like leaves; and where they most
                                    abound,
Much fruit of sense beneath is rarely
                                    found.
                    ~Alexander Pope

Travel in the younger sort is part of education, in the elder, a part of experience.
                    ~Francis Bacon

We hold these truths to be self-evident that
all men are created equal, that they are endowed by their Creator with certain unalienable Rights…
                    ~Declaration of Independence

How do I love thee? Let me count the ways.
                    ~Elizabeth Barrett Browning

One kind word can warm three winter
months.
                    ~Japanese Proverb

He who knows only his side of the
case, knows little of that.
                    ~John Stuart Mill

A written word is the choic-
est of relics.
                    ~Henry David Thoreau

I have a dream…
                    ~Martin Luther King

My soul has grown deep like the rivers.
                    ~Langston Hughes

I hear America singing…
                    ~Walt Whitman

There is no Frigate like a Book
To take us Lands away.
                    ~Emily Dickinson

The limits of my language are the
limits of my world.
                    ~Ludwig Wittgenstein

I dream of lost vocabularies that might express some of what we no longer can.
                    ~Jack Gilbert

Fairness is not given. It is made.
~Anton Treuer

Language is wine upon the lips.
~Virginia Woolf

I am always sorry when a language is lost, because languages are pedigrees of nations.
~Samuel Johnson

A language embraces not just words, phrases, and sentences but the very culture of a people. These represent objects and thoughts, feelings and events, insights and discoveries, people, and animals, in the daily lives of a specific people, living in a specific geographic location, a given period of time. Language represents a way of life, values, and changes of a society. The language of a people, therefore, lets us into the nature, personality, and reality of their culture and existence.

A. Roots and Branches

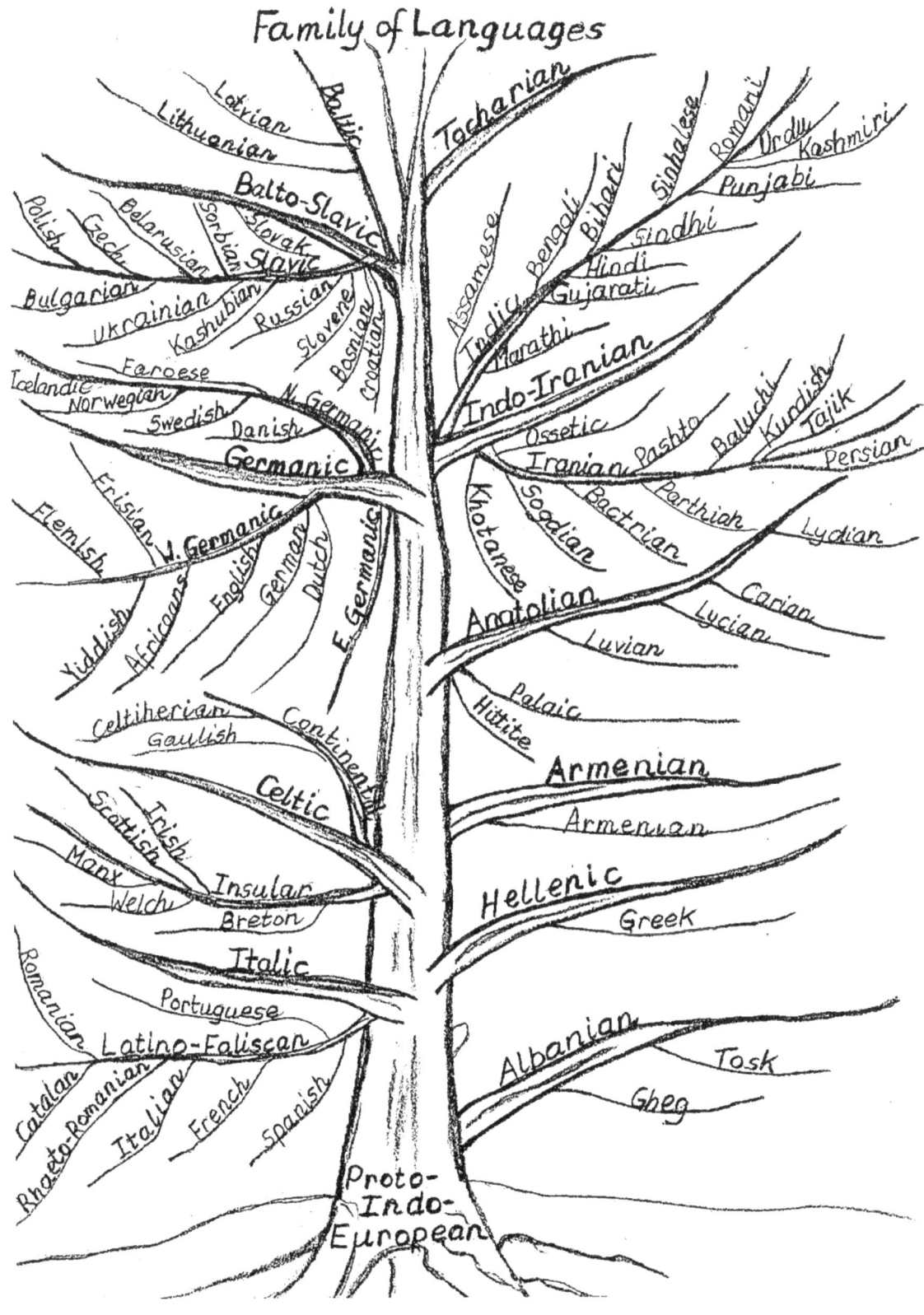

Chapter 1
WHAT IS LANGUAGE?

Many linguists today think of language as basically originating in images, feelings, thoughts, and expressions that consist primarily of human sounds, symbols, and gestures. Transposed into words, they represent objects and thoughts, feelings and events, people, animals, and so on. Expressed in phrases and sentences, these expand into language people use to interact with each other, voice and exchange feelings and information, to think, reason, and develop ideas. Thus, some consider language a system of communication. Eventually, people devised written forms to record their language. Speech patterns and habits, along with speech sounds and gestures as well as written expression of a language, are intricately interwoven with the culture in which they exist, including its social order, history and geography, commerce and industry, religion and system of values and beliefs.

Therefore, when we study a language, or history of a language, we are not only studying the words but the culture of a specific people, their way of expressing or doing things, their way of living, their values, their community. The study of a language allows us into the nature and reality of their culture and existence. Even when languages are related and have the same or similar origins, there are considerable differences that have made each language unique over distance and time. Regional dialects, including some idioms and differentiated use of words, colloquialisms, slang, non-standard use of English are all versions of language use within the language that account for its variations in their immediate communities.

The scientific study of language is called *linguistics*. It studies human language, its origin, nature, reality, structure, and historical development. In this respect, linguistics has established several categories, such as philology, morphology, syntax, semantics, phonology, phonetics, phonemics, and etymology, among others. Each of these, then, concerns itself specifically with one particular aspect of language. Philology is the study of language through literature. Morphology studies words, their formation and grammatical meaning. Syntax studies the arrangement of words into clauses and sentences. Semantics studies the meaning of words and their changes. Phonology is the study of speech sounds, including the history and changes of these sounds as they exist in a given language or in related languages. Phonetics is the study of speech sounds of a language as they represent written symbols. Phonemics is the study of phonemes, the smallest distinguishable speech sounds in a language. Finally, etymology is concerned with the origin of words, their changes, derivations, and transmission from language to language, and their cognates.

In addition to these basic categories of linguistics, other categories have come into existence, particularly in more recent times, and others will undoubtedly be added in the future.

Thus, language is made up of human sounds, symbols, and gestures in the context of a particular cultural setting. Writing is used to represent language. Linguistics, the study of language, is concerned with origin, nature, reality, structure, and historical development of language. In this respect, linguistics has established numerous categories of study over the course of history.

Chapter 2
HOW DO WE ACQUIRE AND DEVELOP LANGUAGE?

So many of us take language for granted. After all, it is such a natural part of our lives and exists, for the most part, unconsciously. It is not until we are called upon to write that we begin to hesitate, and when we are asked to analyze language structure, we may struggle altogether, unless we have learned something about grammar. Most of us don't think about the fact that the English language we use today developed over several centuries, with roots established well before that, having developed speech sounds and formed basic language structures, likely, in the dawn of human existence. Language changes occur as the culture using it experiences changes in its way of life and language usage, resulting in such language changes as sound shifts, changes in its structural aspects, and changes in spelling of words, for example. When we take a closer look, we further discover some words were used differently in earlier times, some became archaic or obsolete, others have added meanings to those already existing, while increasing numbers of new words are added to the language every year, particularly in recent times.

It makes sense that languages in general, including English, would change when we take into consideration how the world has progressed from prehistoric times to the present. Human subsistence has progressed from hunting, fishing, and food gathering to agriculture, from bartering to trade, from hand-made products to mechanized production, from industrialization to technological advances and has done so at an accelerating speed. Social, political, and economic changes and conditions within countries, then, brought about further changes. Countries, variously, moved from status of groups and tribes to that of kingdoms and monarchies, to countries and nations, dictatorships and totalitarianisms, democracies and nation states, many eventually espousing a more global approach.

All of these developments create and add new concepts represented by vocabulary and language features, rendering some older ones outdated or politically incorrect. All we have to do is look at literature or documents belonging to different periods in history to notice changes in grammar, spelling, word use and meaning, words that have disappeared, or words that suddenly appear. And because life and culture keep on changing, language exists in a constant flux. This leaves linguists with the task of studying language, trace and analyze its components and categorize them to explain their use. Modern linguists took it upon itself to reconstruct some origins, while tracing sound shifts and other changes that occurred over the centuries and continues to do so into the future.

Origin

Since we have no direct evidence as to how language originated, we can only conjecture as to its beginnings. We assume that spoken language began in prehistoric times, though we have no exact evidence as to how this played itself out. We can assume speaking preceded writing. Most of the early evidence collected about language comes from written sources. These sources do not go back far enough in time, however, to give us information about the beginnings of language. Yet, it is safe to assume that as language evolved in prehistoric times, the spoken word preceded that of written symbols and expressions.

The ancient Greeks, in the 5th and 4th centuries B. C. made the first known speculations as to the origins of language. Plato advocated that language arose out of reality or nature, and Aristotle postulated that language came about by mutual agreement. It is conceivable human beings attached certain sounds to specific concrete and abstract things of the environment. And when they used the same sounds repeatedly and with other human beings in the same reference, communication was established. Perhaps this communication was augmented by gestures and body movements, even actions. As time went by, more sounds were added, eventually to the point of constructing sentences. But to be understood, these structures had to be consistent and follow a given order.

It is, also, conceivable that language began in a manner similar to the way an infant learns to speak. Usually, among the first words an infant will utter are those associated with the people who care for him or her, like "mom" and "dad" or the like. Some of these, like "mama" and "papa" or versions thereof, cross languages and cultures. Other early words may be associated with food or something the child notices or wants. The child imitates and practices speech sounds it hears from those who care for him or her. This language acquisition occurs primarily in an unconscious process. As the child grows older, he or she will gradually add other words which the child hears and which are important to him or her in some way. Eventually, the child learns to speak in phrases and simple sentences. More complex sentences are usually formed when the child gets older. Further, an individual's language growth will continue through school, work, and throughout life as well as through other associations, additional education, and reading.

Interestingly, much of our thought process begins in images. For example, sometimes, when we want to speak of an object or place, the word fails us, yet we have a clear image of it in our mind to the point where we can describe it in every detail, saying, the word "is on the tip of my tongue." Though our explanation may be cliché, it is a clear image in itself. Or, we forget a person's name, while we clearly see his or her face before us. As poet, many of my poetic lines come to me in images first, images that become transposed into words. Conversely, as artist, when I am attracted to a visual image, there often is a story waiting to be told or written.

The fact that we think in images first has important implications for language learning. Thus, when teaching a word, it is more effective to associate the word with the image. Similarly, when teaching a world language, for instance, showing an image or picture of something and then associating it with the word, its sound, and then its spelling, instead of giving a word for a word, as used to be the practice, will result in far greater retention on part of the student.

This also accounts for the fact that before earliest symbols of writing surfaced, cave drawings depicting stories about animals and hunt, appeasement of elements and life long ago, may be considered evidence that drawing preceded writing. Drawings then led the way to pictographs, an early form of writing. It is important, therefore, to keep in mind that language is image, then speech sound. Writing, thus, is representation of speech sounds. And once acquired, these become unconscious in whatever rendition or language the individual has learned them.

Early known people to use symbols to represent speech sounds were the Canaanites around 1500 B. C. From this, the Phoenicians derived their alphabet, making changes and additions. The Greeks, in turn, took the Phoenician alphabet, making a number of changes. The Romans, then, used a version of the Greek alphabet that included changes made by the Etruscans and the Romans themselves (Am. Herit. 52). The Western world, greatly influenced by Latin for several centuries, eventually adopted the Roman alphabet.

Emergence of Grammar

The addition of written symbols, of course, made it possible for people to develop a written representation of language, allowing them to pass on written messages, create literature and a variety of texts.

In time, we find the beginning and development of grammatical analysis, of classification and structure. In the early 4th century B. C. Greek literature and philosophy brought about the study of grammar, beginning with Plato and Aristotle who separated nouns, verbs, and connectives (Swiggers 532i). By the 1st century B. C., the Greeks had established a grammar that served as model for Latin grammar.

In the early period A. D., much of the study of grammar and writing had religious incentive. This was also true of the grammatical studies done by the Hebrews. It was certainly true of Latin grammar which dominated Europe through the Middle Ages. As a matter of fact, during this time, Latin remained the official, religious, and scientific language of much of the Western world. And Greek and Hebrew were still considered important languages. Yet unversed in these classic languages, the great numbers of ordinary people primarily spoke their individual languages and dialects in which they carried on their daily business.

At the end of the Middle Ages, Latin began to lose its dominance. Throughout early history, into the Middle Ages and beyond, language existed primarily in the spoken word; the ability to read and write was a sign of the privileged or ruling classes. Few books were in existence, because manuscripts and books had to be written by hand. In the Western world, most of this writing was done by monks in monasteries.

The 15th century brought about important developments that initiated new thinking and approaches. The invention of the printing press by Johannes Gutenberg made books more readily available. The translation of the bible from Latin into German and English and other languages established a more compelling incentive and need to read and write. With the coming of the Renaissance and the increasing importance of individual languages, people of different languages began to develop their own grammars, dictionaries, and lexicons. Yet Greek- and Latin-derived grammars served as models and foundations for the grammatical analyses of other Western languages. That explains why even today grammatical terms are generally Greek and Latin derived, although the systems of grammar they describe, may not be of Greek or Latin origin at all. This is certainly the case in English as well as in German, for example.

The Beginning of Modern Linguistics

In the 17th and 18th centuries, people began to look at the historical development of language, attempting to establish relationships between languages. They hoped to find a common ancestor for all languages but without success. Nevertheless, some of the greatest fundamental advances in the study of linguistics were initiated at this time. The German, Franz Bopp, found a link between Sanskrit and the languages of Europe. The Dane, Rasmus Rask, found correspondences between Western languages. The German, Jacob Grimm, and others pursued comparative grammars. Because of developments like these, the Indo-European family of languages that came into focus was more recently renamed Proto-Indo-European.

It was in the nineteenth century that linguistics became a scientific discipline. Language studies continue into the 21st century with the addition of categories as they are developed over time. Some of the major categories involved are the philosophy of language, theory of knowledge and psychology.

21st Century Perspective

The past brought developments of language into the 21st century as living language continues to develop and grow right along with everyday usages, events, new discoveries, and inventions. These continually influence new ways of thinking, observing, experimenting, discovering, researching. Most recently, scientific and technological developments have added greatly to our knowledge base and language stock as have new Scientific and psychological insights gained, frequently resulting in changes of lifestyle. Each category creates its own new terms and vocabulary in the process. As each age is marked by such contributions, it adds to the stock of vocabulary from which we draw today. These advances are like steps of a pyramid, the pyramid of human progress as reflected in language, each step the foundation for the next one, as we continue to build the pyramid. Because of the on-going interconnectedness of the Western world and todays' global existence, expedited by technology, epochs have brought about shared advances and continue to do so at a greater scale, bringing changes and additions that affect languages, keeping them constantly in flux.

We are not mere witnesses of but active participants in this process of change, particularly when we work in or engage in fields that help create new vocabulary and terms. Since the late 20th century, we have added social/political terms such as *multicultural, politically correct, diversity, Merica, afrofuturism, peoplekind, glamping,* and *toxic*, to name a few. Technology has contributed *World Wide Web, e-mail, texting, tweet, viral, to friend*, and *clickbait*, for example. A children's author even contributed the word *scrumdiddlyumptious*. These are but a few terms reflecting changes we were born into or grew into in our daily lives. The development of language and its changes is not just an illusive process led by linguists and intellectuals, as it includes the general population's expressions and usage, including teen usage, even slang and colloquialisms. When use of newly coined words becomes widespread over several years, these are absorbed into the language, according to the *Oxford English Dictionary* which publishes several hundred new words each year.

We notice differences in language quite readily when comparing some of our grandparents' favorite expressions to those of our parents and, in turn, to our own, and, further, to those of our children. In the use of language, we discover some interesting generational variations. For example, in the 1960s, the word "ain't" was not to be whispered within earshot of an English teacher, it is said; by the 1970s it was listed in the dictionary; in 2011, it was still listed but considered nonstandard. For older generations, the first response to the word "gay" may bring up the meaning "lively;" for younger generations, the first response will likely be "sexual orientation." In the 1940s the word "swell" was a popular expression, as many old movies reveal. In later 20th century, the word "bad" expressed approval, followed by "super." In the early 21st century, the word "sweet" occupied that spot among the young. Many of the words and expressions we use are like flags of different times and influences that produced them. Thus, in order to stay current, we ride the wave of these changes so as not to be left behind, outdated or worse in some cases, open to ridicule, resentment, or, in its extreme, loss of credibility.

It is easy to see how language acquisition plays a vital role in our lives. And because of its unconscious nature, it is spontaneous, and can be surprising in its effect for a variety of reasons.

We acquire language in a number of ways, reacting to our environment which determines the extent to which we learn to use language. Most notably, children learn by imitation. Sometimes children repeat words, expressions, even sentences they have not yet learned to understand, causing amusement or embarrassment for older siblings and adults. Whatever the language spoken around the child by parents, siblings, playmates and friends that is the language the child will learn and use. The choice and variety of words, the ability to verbalize, express ideas and feelings, all are influenced by the people and experiences in the child's world. If a child is exposed to language variety and complexity, perhaps even another language, the more likely the child will develop more extensive speech habits and good language skills.

The idea that some languages are harder to learn than others is a myth. Exposure to good language models and opportunity to learn in a variety of exposures are the important factors here. A child born into any language has the opportunity to learn that language with all its given intricacies to the extent the daily environment offers. For that reason, language immersion schools offer students the opportunity to learn a second language in much the same fashion as the first, for instance.

Reading is a particularly valuable source of language learning. This can begin when the child is young and parents and siblings read to him or her. It helps pave the way for school later on. At school, students discover new worlds of meaning in subjects, such as, mathematics, language arts, world languages, the sciences, social studies, the arts, sports, computer science, business and technical education, etc., all associated with reading and new vocabulary. Ordinarily, we do not think of these courses as increasing our vocabulary, but their specialized terms may open new worlds of reasoning and participation for many. When we progress from basic schooling to technical education and higher education to job, occupation or profession, we enter these worlds and their specific vocabularies and ways of thinking. Furthermore, each group that we belong to, depending on purpose or function, from gardening clubs to sports clubs, political associations to social groups, book clubs to art groups, nature clubs to science clubs, and so on, also contributes its own particular vocabulary to the language we use in our daily lives.

In the world at large, the social, political, economic environment, and international scenes as well as trends, events, new discoveries, etc., mark the vocabulary and terminology of any given language, time and geographic area. In this respect, the computer has added a great deal of convenience and reality in terms of personal as well as global accessibility, both inviting the use of and addition of new aspects of language, including crossover vocabulary. Therefore, the daily environment affecting our language is expanding as well and is rich in its language offerings.

The idea that we know all we need to know after we graduate from high school or even college has long been outdated, just like the horse and buggy, therefore. Learning is not just for the young but remains, increasingly so, a life-long process of which initial schooling is only the foundation. The acquisition of language is an important element in this process. When we learn about new things in the world around us, we expand our language range and ability to think at the same time.

Over the ages, it became increasingly clear to statesmen, philosophers, religious leaders, and intellectuals alike that a good education, at the base of which are good language skills, is essential for productive and positive participation in the activities of individual citizens, indispensable to the economic, political, social, and cultural well-being of a country's population as a whole. This realization eventually culminated in moving education from primarily the privileged classes to the establishment of compulsory public education beginning in the 19th century.

Conclusion

We do not know the exact origin of language and can only conjecture about its beginnings. Yet over the course of written history, we can trace many of the developments of language to today's use. Linguistics uncovers many of the intricacies and changes of language occurring over time. Language as a system of communication is always in flux, both orally and written, existing in the living expression of a culture. We find this evidenced in changing pronunciation, spelling, and meaning of words, or words that have become obsolete or archaic, and by the addition of new words. Some words and expressions may be coined by people like scientists, researchers, philosophers, politicians, inventors, industries, and other individuals or groups of influence. At other times, they may be directed in a deliberate move by contemporary language authorities, and at still other times, these changes may occur through popular usage. Often these changes slip in almost unnoticed by the casual user. Different generations create their influx of popular expressions. Consequently, we can often identify a group or generation by their word choices and expressions, specialized vocabulary, even by their sentence structure. Our language continues to develop, change, and grow in the current of time, progress, and culture. It remains always in flux.

Chapter 3
THE INDO-EUROPEAN FAMILY OF LANGUAGES

To appreciate the English language as it is spoken today, it is helpful to regard it in its historical setting from which it evolved along with the other Indo-European languages to which it is related. The Indo-European family of languages, to which English belongs and to which most of the languages of Europe and the Western world belong, originally filtered through migrations of people from areas south and east of today's Europe, such as India, Afghanistan, and Iran, westward to Europe. These language groups settled in Europe, arriving approximately 20,000 to 12,000 years ago, establishing themselves in approximately the areas these languages occupy today as countries. After they settled, they lived, initially, in relative isolation, accounting for their lingual and cultural variations.

The scope of the relationship between the Indo-European languages was not determined until relatively recent times, however. In the 18th century, the study of Sanskrit contributed important insights into the study of comparative linguistics. This ancient language came to the foreground during that century's colonialism and mercantilism. Up to that point, linguists were primarily aware of similarities between the classical languages of Greek and Latin and the other languages in Europe, namely Italic, Germanic, and Slavic. But when Sanskrit came into the picture, comparisons were made, leading to significant findings and connections. The German philologist Franz Bopp discovered these in his comparative studies of the grammar of Sanskrit, Greek, Latin and Germanic languages. His study allowed scholars of the 19th century to determine that these and some of the other languages belonged to the same family of languages which they termed Indo-European (*Am. Herit.* 2024-2025). Similarities between these Indo-European languages exist in sounds, spelling, words of common origin as well as in language structures.

Initially, the Indo-European languages were very similar to one another (McNeill 680), derived from a common ancestor which was eventually reconstructed and named Proto-Indo-European. Over time, these languages developed in different directions. In the European branch, the Germanic languages split into three groups: East Germanic, now extinct; West Germanic, from which we derive English, High German, Dutch, Yiddish, among others; and North Germanic, from which we derive most of the languages of Scandinavia. Latin became the ancestor of Italic languages, such as Italian, Spanish, Portuguese, etc., with Latin itself declining and fading from use. The Slavic languages branched out, after migrations to eastern and central Europe, forming three branches, West Slavic, South Slavic and East Slavic, embracing such languages as Polish, Bulgarian, and Russian, respectively. The Celtic languages, divided into two branches, Continental and Insular. The Hellenic branch of the Indo-European family of languages consists only of modern Greek.

The main divisions of the Asian branch are Indo-Iranian, whose surviving languages branch out into Indic and Iranian with such languages as Bengali and Hindi and Persian and Pashto, respectively. Two additional branches of the Asian languages are Anatolian and Tocharian.

The chart on the next page, roughly, outlines the Indo-European family of languages. It contains primarily a listing of the main language divisions with the respective languages below them. For obvious reasons, emphasis here is on the European branch of these languages, to which English belongs, and languages spoken today, omitting some of the intermediate stages of development. The Asiatic languages appear primarily in their main language categories. The Indo-European languages can be divided into nine main language families. These families branch off, in many cases, into other subdivisions until they become the last listing on the chart.

Family of Languages
PROTO-INDO-EUROPEAN

Balto-Slavic
    Baltic> Old Prussian, Lithuanian, Latvian

    Slavic> Sorbian, Polish, Slovak, Czech, Slovene, Serbo-Croatian, Macedonian, Bulgarian, Old Church Slavonic, Ukrainian, Byelorussian, Russian

Germanic
    West Germanic> English, German, Frisian, Yiddish, Dutch> Afrikaans, Flemish

    North Germanic> Icelandic, Faroese, Norwegian, Swedish, Danish

Celtic
    Insular> Irish Gaelic, Scottish Gaelic, Manx

    Continental> Welsh, Cornish, Breton

Italic
    Latino> Latin> Portuguese, Spanish, Catalan, Provençal, French, Italian, Rhaeto-Romanian, Romanian

Albanian
    Gheg, Tosk

Hellenic
    Greek

Armenian
    Armenian

Anatolian
    Lydian, Carian Lycian, Luvian, Palaic, Hittite

Indo-Iranian

    Indic>Sanskrit> Assamese, Bengali, Bihari, Singhalese, Marathi, Gujarati, Hindi, Sindhi, Punjabi, Urdu, Romany

    Iranian> Tajik, Pashto, Baluchi, Kurdish, Persian (Farsi)

Tocharian

It is of interest to note how the population numbers of the Indo-European languages compare in the pool of world languages by the end of the 20th century. The table of the *Ethnologue: Languages of the World* ranks the "Top 100 Languages by Population." A distribution of these figures highlighting primarily the Indo-European languages is listed below. The ranking for each language is given, followed by the principal country or countries in which it is spoken, the corresponding population figures, and ranking according to world listing of languages.

Language and Ranking	Country	Population
1. Spanish second after Chinese	Spain, Mexico, Central and South America	332,000,000
2. English third	U.S.A., United Kingdom, Canada, Australia	322,000,000
3. Bengali fourth	Bangladesh	189,000,000
4. Hindi fifth	India	182,000,000
5. Portuguese sixth	Portugal, Brazil	170,000,000
6. Russian seventh	Russia	170,000,000
7. German ninth after Japanese	Germany, Austria, part of Switzerland, Liechtenstein, Luxembourg	98,000,000
8. French Thirteenth	France, Belgium, part or Switzerland, part of Canada	72,000,000
9. Marati seventeenth	India	64,783,000

Language and Ranking	Country	Population
10. Polish twentieth	Poland	44,000,000
11. Ukrainian twenty-fourth	Ukraine	41,000,000
12. Italian twenty-seventh	Italy, part of Switzerland	37,000,000
13. Romanian thirty-sixth	Romania	26,000,000
14. Serbo-Croatian forty-fourth Serbia, Montenegro, Croatia, Bosnia, Herzegovina	(formerly Yugoslavia)	21,000,000
15. Dutch forty-eighth	Netherlands	20,000,000
16. Greek seventy-fourth	Greece	12,000,000
17. Bulgarian eighty-eighth	Bulgaria	9,000,000
18. Swedish eighty-ninth	Sweden	9,000,000

Conclusion

The study of linguistics is relatively new and led to the conclusion that the Indo-European languages can be traced back to a single ancestor. This ancestor was reconstructed and named Proto-Indo-European. Over the course of time, languages branched out from this ancestor, forming the Indo-European family of languages. These languages changed over time and branched out into other languages, while others became extinct, giving us the various languages in use today. Their relationship is based on a relative similarity of sounds, spelling, words of common origin and grammatical structures. The closeness of the relationship depends on the language family each language is a part of. Spoken languages continue to exist in a constant state of flux and have continued to develop and change within their language groups over the centuries. The location of some of these languages has also changed and/or expanded world-wide, increasing their population numbers, while others have remained, more or less, in their place of original settlement, keeping population numbers relatively moderate to low by comparison.

How does the relationship of these languages compare in terms of words they each use? The chapter Cognates in Indo-European Languages will address the answer.

Chapter 4
Cognates in Indo-European Languages

Cognates are words of related languages that come from the same root. The Indo-European languages share some words that are the same or similar in their form and meaning, although they may have changed over time due to changes in pronunciation, sound shifts, spelling changes or change in meaning.

Below is a list of cognates for comparison. It is interesting to note the similarities and differences. We can assume that these words are the historical survivors of Indo-European roots. The Indo-European words have been reconstructed and are listed here as well (Algeo 90-91).

COGNATE NOUNS

English	father	mother	brother	night	foot
German	Vater	Mutter	Bruder	Nacht	Fuß
French	père	mère	frère	nuit	pied
Spanish	padre	madre	hermano	noche	pie
Latin	pater	māter	frāter	noctis	pedis
Greek	patēr	mētēr	phrātēr	nuktos	podos
Russian	otez	mat'	brat	noch'	podu
Sanskrit	pitar-	mātar	bhrātar-	naktam	pad-
Indo-Eur.	pətēr-	*māter-	*bhrāter-	*nokwt-	*men(ōt)-

Note the close correspondences in spelling between the English and German words on the chart. Again, close correspondences between French, Spanish, and Latin as well as Greek words exist. Also, there is a close correspondence of the word night between all of these languages. Interestingly, words such as mama and papa, though not listed here, exist alike in many languages, such as English, German (where they are capitalized), Spanish, French (with a slight variation), Russian, among others.

Following is a list of numbers 1-10 and 100 from various Indo-European languages (Algeo 94). They are grouped by the language families to which they belong. The correspondences of spelling between the members within each language family give an indication of their close relationship. But even between each language group, spelling correspondences, though to a lesser degree, still exist.

COGNATE NUMBERS

Germanic:

ENGLISH	GERMAN	DUTCH	DANISH	**Reconstructed Indo-European**
one	eins	een	en	*oinos
two	zwei	twee	to	*dwō
three	drei	drie	tre	*treyes
four	vier	vier	fire	*kwetwor
five	fünf	vijf	fem	*penkwe
hundred	hundert	honderd	hundrede	*kmtom

Italic: **Hellenic:**

LATIN	ITALIAN	FRENCH	SPANISH	GREEK
unus	uno	un	uno	heis
duo	due	deux	dos	duo
trēs	tre	trois	tres	treis
quattuor	quattro	quatre	cuatro	tettares
quīnque	cinque	cinq	cinco	pente
centum	cento	cent	ciento	hekaton

Slavic:		**Baltic:**	**Iranic:**
RUSSIAN	POLISH	LITHUANIAN	PERSIAN
odin	jeden	vienas	yek
dva	dwa	du	do
tri	trzy	trys	se
chetyre	cztery	keturi	cahar
pyat'	pięć	penki	panj
sto	sto	šimtas	sad

As we can see, many similarities exist between the numbers within each language family and to a lesser degree, between the different language families that we can trace to the reconstructed Indo-European roots. For instance, in the Germanic languages, the numbers nine, ten and 100 are very close. Similar correspondences exist in the Italic languages with the numbers 1, 9, 10 and 100. When it comes to the language families, we find correspondences between Italic and Greek numbers, particularly 2, 3 and 6 and between Germanic and Greek numbers 1, 3, 5, 6, and 8. The correspondences between Slavic and Greek, though generally less obvious, are quite evident in the numbers 2, 3 and 6.

One more thing: Not all words that are spelled alike, or even the same, in different Indo-European languages are cognates. Many of them are borrowings. The English word *restaurant*, for example, is *Restaurant* in German and *restaurant* in Dutch. All three are borrowings and come from the French. In a similar situation, we have the word *quahvah* from the Arabic from which came *qahvhe* in Turkish, then became *caffè* in Italian (Am. Herit.); in French it became *cafè*. From French it was borrowed and became English *coffee*, Dutch *koffie*, and German *Kaffee*.

Conclusion

The Indo-European languages share many cognates, words that are derived from the same root and are similar in form and meaning. This is particularly true of words that exist inside a given language family. But cognates exist between language families as well. Because cognates cross between language families, linguists stipulate these words come from a single Indo-European root, evidence, in part, that the languages are related. At the same time, it is important to keep in mind that not all words that have similar or even the same spelling are cognates.

Exactly, how does English fit into this picture? What are the characteristics that set it apart from other languages? These questions will be addressed next.

Chapter 5
HISTORICAL PERSPECTIVE AND THE ENGLISH LANGUAGE

Members of the Indo-European language families share a long unfolding of historical progress. As speakers of these languages existed in separate environments, they developed each their own particular language identity with its own musical quality or phonetic system, rules of usage and grammar, vocabulary and expressions or idioms peculiar to their environment and cultural activities, reflecting their daily lives as well as political and religious preferences and alliances. Within languages, dialectal variations also developed, creating more diversity of language expression within countries and beyond. By the same token, some countries belonging to the Italic language family, such as Spain or Italy, became predominantly Catholic, while Germany's population eventually divided predominantly into Protestants in the north and Catholics in the south. Britain dealt with its own religious differences, eventually establishing the Church of England. Many of these developments held ramifications for language, bible translations, and the move toward literacy.

Each group existed, dominated not only by the religious leanings of its rulers but by its own political and economic makeup as well. Language borders, more often than not, resulted in political or national borders. Since the Indo-European languages are descended from one ancestor, now reconstructed as Proto-Indo-European, however, they retain some common aspects, including, for most of them, the alphabet, related vocabularies and a similarity of grammatical systems. The closeness of that relationship depends on where in the language family groupings they belong, as we have seen. Since these language groups exist in today's countries or states, more or less, they shared some common historical developments from which they benefited. Yet their relationships have remained intact, despite conflict and competition frequently arising, like sibling rivalry, alliances forming according to political or economic circumstances or preferences.

Borrowings of words from other languages allowed them to keep up with each other's ideas, advancements and changes. In today's languages, borrowings of words from other languages have become even more commonplace and widespread, with technology at heart of communication and transportation to nearly any part of the world instantly, safely, and comfortably. Thus, whether personal or national, business or recreational, economic or political, religious or philosophical, our interactions are moving increasingly forward on a global scale.

Historically, some of the Indo-European languages either dominated or exerted their influence, depending on political, social, economic, and cultural influences of given periods. Greek produced early philosophies, literature, and grammatical models. Latin, now considered a "dead" language, wound its influence into modern times as language of the church, literature, and science. Many of its words and terms have found their way into other languages that borrowed or absorbed them altogether. And since the earliest grammatical system recorded was established in Latin, the myth still exists among some that grammar, per se, is of Latin origin, when in reality only the Latin terms have been borrowed to describe grammatical systems of other Indo-European languages.

While Latin dominated in the early centuries of modern history, French enjoyed great popularity in the Middle Ages, when France was in a position of power and cultural influence. Moreover, during the reign of Louis XIV, the popularity of French grew in Europe not only as language of diplomats, the courts, and the "cultured" but as that of scientists as well. Its influence and popularity, not surprisingly, survived well into the 20th century. For the English language, Anglo-Saxon, Norse, and French were of particular influence, as we shall see in the chapter detailing the history of the English language. Other languages, such as German, borrowed many French words that exist today side by side with their German counterparts. But in the course of developments, German took its turn influencing other languages with vocabulary in such fields as science, philosophy and psychology, for instance. Today, English remains at the head of the popularity list of not only German but on the international scene in general.

Often, people looked on the borders separating countries of the Indo-European languages as much as a protective territorial necessity as a hindrance to free movement for peaceful, economic, and cultural pursuits. The search for unifying elements gradually increased into modern times, particularly after the consequences of two devastating world wars and the potential nuclear threat in the future.

People sought common ground in their communication with each other. Already in the late 19th century, attempting to find a common European language, the Polish linguist Ludovic Zamenhof, invented Esperanto. This language was made up of various Western Indo-European languages. It was streamlined to contain a simplified grammar and vocabulary, intended to be easy to learn and convenient to use. In 1954, it generated renewed interest when it was accepted as being in agreement with the purpose of UNESCO. However, Esperanto never reached quite the intended prospect of being the one international language. Nevertheless, it is taught in some schools and universities and is used in educational and scientific information and periodicals in various countries of the world but in limited scope. This international language still in use today has only about one million speakers (Tonkin 583).

While in principle, the idea of this neutrally created language is appealing, the shortcoming is that it is not grounded in cultural growth and development. That is to say, no one grows up with it naturally, speaking the language in the home environment as part of the main culture and on through time when it becomes part of developments at large.

Today, if there is a universal language, not only in the western world but in the global community, it is undoubtedly English. Its use in the United States as well as in countries like Canada, United Kingdom, and Australia, for instance, takes in large population numbers that certainly have a bearing. Beyond that, there are additional reasons for its popularity. For one, English lends itself well to expression in all areas of pursuit with uncomplicated vocabulary and short, simple sentences, without compromising meaning, despite mixed vocabulary and varied spelling of words. It is considered by many a practical business language. The electronic age has added to this perspective, since so much of the computer language is generated in English which quickly finds its way into other languages. Even German, for example, a language easily suited to the creation of its own new vocabulary, borrows large numbers of popular words from English at present, so that German, at times, may sound like a variation of English itself.

However, because of the variety of languages spoken in Europe and because translations are easily open to errors, inaccuracies, and misunderstandings, these countries cope with the need for better communication by promoting the study of other languages in addition to their own. Often these languages are those of bordering countries. Most of the European countries today require that school age populations study at least one foreign language. Depending on the level of schooling and the country, the requirement may involve two languages or more, frequently including Latin. English will almost certainly be one of the languages required, with German a close second, and such languages as French, Russian, and more recently Spanish, not far behind.

Furthermore, the shuffle of borders due to wars and conflict over territory as well as immigrants, refugees and migrants has created pockets of cultural minorities speaking languages other than the official one. This is the case with the German cultural minorities in Russia, Poland, and Luxembourg, for instance. In Switzerland, the existence of four separate official languages, German, French, Italian and Romansch, gives equal recognition to each language, although German occupies position of official language. Similarly, in Canada, we find English spoken in most of the country, while French is primarily spoken in the province of Quebec. Of course, languages like Chinese and Arabic are just beginning to gain favor in school curriculums in some of the western countries due, in part, to a new population influx of migrants. In the United States new immigrants, particularly those from south of the border, from Africa and Asia enjoy the help of many businesses and organizations that offer translations rendered in their specific native tongues.

Because of the cultural activities and experiences associated with language, learning a second language or more opens other doors of understanding, not only to the people of another culture but, in the process, to the world of our own by exposure to new concepts, perspectives, and comparisons. This leads us to see the world and ourselves with a new awareness and expanded view. But most immediately, we develop better comprehension of and appreciation for our own language. Moreover, we find ourselves better equipped to interact successfully with people of other cultures and their diversity.

What, then, is the story of English? The next section will answer that question.

B. The Story of English

Old English
To Hrothgar was granted glory in war,
Success in battle…
~Beowulf

Middle English
Whan that Aprille with hise shores soote
The droghte of March hath perced to theroote…
~Chaucer

Early Modern English
Shall I compare thee to a summer's day?
~Shakespeare

Modern English
We the People of the United States, in order to form a more perfect Union, establish Justice insure domestic Tranquility, provide for the common Defence, promote the general Welfare…

This is my letter to the world
That never wrote to Me –
~Emily Dickinson

Psychology can be brought to bear upon the study of literature.
~C. G. Jung

The Theory of Relativity
~ Albert Einstein

Chapter 6
THE BEGINNING: OLD ENGLISH

To understand the seeming contradictions in the English language, it is helpful to understand the various influences that comprise it. As member of the Germanic branch of the Indo-European Family of languages, English has in common its word stock, inflectional endings of words, word accent, the alphabet, grammatical structures, and the Great Vowel Shift. Modern English evolved out of the influences of three distinct historical periods, encompassing Old English, Middle English and Modern English.

The Old English period dates from about 450-1100 A. D. The English language came into existence when three Germanic tribes, the Angles, the Saxons, and the Jutes invaded the British Isles in the middle of the 5th century. They conquered the people living there, namely the Celts, and soon established the dialects of their own language as well as their customs. Very few words of the Celtic language remained after the invasion. The new dialects soon spread but did not enjoy equal use. The dialects that eventually prevailed were that of the Angles and particularly that of the West Saxons, the dialect spoken in the area of Wessex. Anglo-Saxon became the foundation of what is called *Old English* today. According to the *American Heritage Dictionary,* the word English can be traced to Old English, *Englisc,* which is derived from *Engle*, traced to Angles.

At the time of the invasion, these Germanic tribes had adopted an alphabet called *runes* which they used from about the 3rd to the 13th century. But because of Rome's influence, the tribes also brought along some knowledge of Latin. As they converted to Christianity, the use of Latin became more prolific, and they began to use the Roman alphabet, with Latin becoming both church and political language of the period, concurrently with the newly emerging Anglo-Saxon language of the people.

Examples of vocabulary entering the language at this time were such common Germanic words as *night, father, son, hand, arm, ring,* and *wind.* We can see their correspondences to other languages of the Germanic group, such as German, as well. In English the word *night,* derived from Germanic *naht,* comes to us from Old English, changing in Middle English to *niht* or *neaht.* The modern High German word *Nacht* is derived from the same Germanic word, *naht.* The English word *father* can be traced to Middle English *fadar,* Old English *fæder,* and Germanic *fadar.* The German counterpart, *Vater,* similarly, is derived from Old High German *fater.* The English word *son* can be traced to Middle English, Old English *sunu,* and Germanic *sunuz* (see *Am. Herit. Dict.*) from which the German word *Sohn* is also derived. The nouns *hand, arm, ring,* and *wind* exist in the same form in English, Dutch as well as in German, the only difference being that nouns are capitalized in German.

Another influence affecting Old English came toward the end of the period, beginning in the 9th century and continuing well into the 10th. England was invaded again, this time by Norsemen from Scandinavia, also a Germanic people. The Danes remained and actually ruled for some time to come, and in the process, introduced many of their Norse words. For example, the word *window* comes to English from Old Norse, *vindauga* which is also related to Modern High German *Wind,* meaning *wind* and Modern High German *Auge* meaning eye, derived from Old High German *ouga.* Another word derived from Old Norse *kidh* is the word *kid.*

English literature had its beginning in this period. Most of the writing was done in monasteries by monks and in Latin. Literature written in English, the vernacular or language of the common people, was in verse and generally passed along orally. Old English literature was an important link with the other Germanic literature written in the rest of Europe. There were, basically, two types of writing, religious poetry and epic poetry. Of this period, the epic poem *Beowulf,* whose author is unknown, is a long narrative poem, filled with heroic deeds, good and evil, and many colorful characters. In it, as in other literature of the time, the mixing of Christian and pagan beliefs is common in this period of transition. The poem was probably composed between 700 and 750 A.D. and takes place in Scandinavia. Its hero comes to the royal court of Denmark, where he helps king Hrothgar against a mysterious foe. Following is a brief excerpt from *Beowulf* in its original form.

Hwæt, we Gar-Dena in geardagum,
þeodcyninga þrym gefrunon,
hu ða æþelingas ellen fremedon!
Oft Scyld Scefing sceaþena þreatum,

monegum mæþum meodosetla ofteah,
egsode eorlas, syððan ærest wearð
feasceaft funden; he þæs frofre gebad,
weox under wolcnum weorðmyndum þah,
oð þæt him æghwylc ymbsittendra
ofer hronrade hyran scolde,
gomban gyldan; þæt wæs god cyning! (Baugh 19)

The following is the modern translation of the excerpt.

Lo, we have heard of the glory in the days of
old of the Spear-Danes, of the kings of the
people, how the athelings did deeds of valor!
Oft Scyld Scefing reft bands of hostile folk,
many a tribe, of their seats in the mead-hall,
terrified earls, after he was first found destitute.
Yet for all that, he lived to know consolation,
prospered on earth and grew rich in honors,
till each of his neighbors over the whale-road
must obey him and pay him tribute.
That was a good king! (Baugh 19-20)

As we can see, the difference between Old and Modern English is great and to the point where most words are either unrecognizable or unfamiliar to today's reader. This is complicated by the fact that some of the letters are no longer in use today. We recognize with certainty only a few words, such as "we", "he", and "in." Still, the last sentence of the selection " þæt wæs god cyning!" gives us some clues as to the modern version of these words. Naturally, the choice of words is affected by the cultural setting and situation being described.

Chapter 7
NEW INFLUENCES: MIDDLE ENGLISH

The Middle English period extends from about 1100-1500. Up to the 11th century, the Danish invaders had dominated England for this extended period of time. But in 1066 the Normans conquered England, bringing about important changes. In the conflicts that continued after the conquest, most of the English nobles were killed and replaced with French nobles. The language spoken at court, therefore, was French, and any remaining English nobles who wanted to be at court had to learn French. This held important consequences for English, although, English remained the language of the common people.

Literature, at this time, was written in three languages, French, Latin and English. French literature was influenced by the elaborate literature of France, its only audience, however, the upper classes. Latin remained the language of knowledge, history, science, and religion. Consequently, most of the literature in Latin was written for and by people of learning and the church. The great masses did not know Latin. English literature was written for the people and enjoyed great variety as well as considerable change over the centuries spanning this period. In the beginning it was of a religious nature. But it eventually became increasingly worldly, moving from adventure to romance, from poetry to prose. Literature was intended to bring enjoyment and entertainment. Oral literature, often presented in songs, was very popular. Toward the end of this period, the drama had its beginning, growing out of the church play, which, in turn, had found its inspiration in Greek plays.

Middle English existed in various dialects, and for that reason, no single pronunciation exists for this period. Middle English is well represented in the work of

Geoffrey Chaucer, the first major English poet. The greatest of his works, and probably his most widely read is the *Canterbury Tales*. The excerpt below, in the original, should give the reader an idea of how English had changed by this point in history.

> A Knyght ther was, and that a worthy man,
> That fro the tyme that he first bigan
> to riden out, he loved chivalrie,
> Trouthe and honour, fredom and curteisie.
> Ful worthy was he in his lordes werre,
> and therto hadde he riden no man ferre
> As wel in cristendom as in hethernesse,
> And evere honoured for his worthynesse. (Baugh 115)

As we can see, in Middle English some of the Old English symbols changed to letters used today. Many words, though recognizable, were spelled differently, however. For example, if we look at Knyght and tyme, we can see that the "y" had changed to "i" in modern *knight* and *time*. "Trouthe" and "honour" today are *truth* and *honor*, "bigan" is *began.* The noun ending "-nesse" is today *–ness,* as in *worthiness,* which also changed the "y" to *i*. We can see the French influence with words, such as "chivalrie" and "curtesie," modern *chivalry* and *courtesy*, that had become part of the English language. Chaucer's Middle English had become much more like Modern English.

Combined Influences

During the first 200 years or so of the Middle English period, English began to show new influences and changes in its transition to Middle English. Important changes in grammar took place. Grammatical gender disappeared, along with the inflectional endings of nouns and adjectives, which still exist in German today, for instance. Present participles also changed their endings. These changes, then, gave way to a standard word order (Bryant 420).

Spelling and the alphabet also changed. For example, Middle English dropped the letters "þ" and "ð," replaced by the letters *th*. The symbol "æ" also disappeared, replaced by the letter *a*. Therefore, Old English "dæ" became middle English *day*. Under the influence of French, spelling changes also occurred. The letters "j, q, v" and "z" were introduced. Later, "ū" became *ou* or *ow*. Therefore, Old English "þū" is Middle English *thou*.

While the English language added an extensive new vocabulary to its existing Anglo-Saxon stock, including such sources as Flemish, Dutch and Low German, the greatest influx of new words came from French as a consequence of the Norman Conquest. Words, such as *cousin, niece, infant, courage, authority, court, reign, clergy, tragedy, romance, entrance, appetite, lemon, boil, flame, declare, leisure*, among many others, made their way into the English language. Latin also made important contributions with words, such as *deterioration, jubilation, distraction, notion, congress, congruent*, among many others.

Chapter 8
EXPANDING LANGUAGE: MODERN ENGLISH

Modern English dates from approximately the 15th century. By this time, the basic components that were to comprise English were set. However, it was during this period that the Great Vowel Shift took place, creating a transition from Middle English to Modern English. The German philologist Jacob Grimm, in his studies during the 18th century, discovered this sound shift among Germanic languages. In English this resulted in phonetic changes of some vowels and the creation of diphthongs of others. From that point on, the languages affected by this vowel shift would progress in different directions.

Highlights of historical events and developments will help us place the changes of the English language in a frame of reference and associate them with literary periods. This will, hopefully, give us a better understanding of some of the ways English changed and developed.

Early Modern English

Early Modern English is placed somewhere between 1500 and 1700. The 16th century was characterized in England by strong rulers. Henry VIII ruled the first part of the century. One of the significant events of his rule was the conflict with the church that led to his separating the Church of England from Rome. The second half followed with the reign of Elizabeth I, 1558-1606, bringing relative stability to the country which she made into a great power.

During this time, the Renaissance, with its humanism, came to England, marking a period of rebirth and growth of spirit and intellect. Learning was no longer primarily through the church. And though it was still not readily accessible to the great masses, it began to draw larger circles among the upper and middle classes. Interest in Latin and Greek was renewed, especially in literature and writing. Many words were borrowed from these languages, with Latin sometimes derived from the Greek. Borrowings from other languages also began to filter into the language.

The 16th century was characterized not only by religious reform, but by developments in science, the arts, literature, and new political and social ideas as well. Many of these ideas led the way to social and political institutions still held in England today and, in turn, found their way to the New World that was just "discovered" in 1492.

The literature of this period contributed to its greatness with its depth, variety, and universality, marking the beginning of Modern English literature. After the fascination with the classics, English returned as the dominant language in Britain. And with the introduction of the printing press by Johannes Gutenberg and brought to England by William Caxton about 1455, books could now be reproduced more easily. After the Reformation in the 16th century, and after some unsuccessful attempts, the Bible's translation into English, at last, found official acceptance. It was an era of new expression. Literary criticism emerged. The drama was revived, becoming the new form of entertainment. Prose began to emerge and poetry, strictly as an oral tradition, found a decline, although it continued to flourish in written form. Some of the greatest English poets came forth during this time, among them Edmund Spenser. This was the period of the dramatist and poet William Shakespeare. In his timeless and universal themes, he explored human ambition and cunning, conflict and tragedy, romance and humor in works, such as *Macbeth, Hamlet, The Tragedy of Othello, A Midsummer Night's Dream, The Merchant of Venice, Romeo and Juliet*, among them. His poetry, including his popular sonnets, still fascinate audiences today.

In the following sonnet, written by Shakespeare, the poet compares a friend to eternal summer. It shows how much Early Modern English had changed from Middle English. The modern reader can readily appreciate and understand the language. Still, some differences exist in the use of words, images, and word order. We find the pronouns *thee* and *thou* for today's *you*, *thy* for *your*, the verb forms *hath* for *has* and *art* for *are*.

Shall I compare thee to a summer's day?
Thou art more lovely and more temperate:
Rough winds do shake the darling buds of May,

And summer's lease hath all too short a date:
Sometime too hot the eye of heaven shines,
And often is his gold complexion dimmed;
And every fair from fair sometimes declines,
By chance, or nature's changing course untrimmed;
But thy eternal summer shall not fade,
Nor lose possession of that fair thou owest;
Nor shall Death brag thou wander'st in his shade,
When in eternal lines to time thou growest:
So long as men can breathe, or eyes can see,
So long lives this, and this gives life to thee.

The 17th Century

The 17th century brought about further changes in England. A struggle between the crown and Parliament ensued during the Commonwealth Period under Oliver Cromwell with Parliament seeking greater power. Consequently, England then moved from military dictatorship to limited monarchy. While England moved from ruler to ruler, Parliament sought a more democratic approach to government, representing primarily the middle class, merchants, the well to do, and upper classes, who wanted greater control over money, taxation, and worship (Baugh 329-33). When Charles II was restored to the throne, religion became a source of conflict because of its various interpretations in this century of reason.

A great variety of literature came about during the 17th century and included religious, philosophical, and scientific writings. The century divides, roughly, into two periods of literature in England. The first half brought forth the Cavalier and Puritan period, with John Milton its most significant writer. Much of his poetry concerned itself with religious topics.

The following selection from *Paradise Lost* by John Milton is close to today's English, despite the use of "didst," archaic in the 21st century.

Of man's first disobedience, and the fruit
Of that forbidden tree, whose mortal taste
Brought death into the world, and all our woe,
With loss of Eden, till one greater Man
Restore us, and regain the blissful seat,
Sing, Heavenly Muse, that on the secret top

Of Oreb, or of Sinai, didst inspire
That shepherd, who first taught the chosen seed
In the beginning how the heavens and earth
Rose out of Chaos…. (Baugh, 411)

The age of new scientific approach, experimentation, and discoveries brought forth, among others, mathematician, physicist and astronomer, Sir Isaac Newton. In the following excerpt, he explains his law of gravitation. Prose finds application in this scientific discussion. While the use of the word *hither* may be considered quaint today, its meaning is clear. The spelling of the word "phaenomena," today *phenomena,* is Late Latin. 21st century American English spelling of *centre* is *center*.

Hitherto we explained the phaenomena of the heavens and of our sea by
the power of gravity, but have not yet assigned the cause of this power. This
is certain, that it must proceed from a cause that penetrates to the very
centres of the sun and planets, without suffering the least diminution of its
force, that operates according to the quantity of the surfaces of the particles
upon which it acts (as mechanical causes used to do), but according to the
quantity of the solid matter which they contain and propagates its virtue on
all sides to immense distances, decreasing always in the duplication portions
of the distances.

Emerging out of the Elizabethan age with the Renaissance interest in learning and new experiences was Francis Bacon, 1561-1626, one of England's great philosophers and essayists of the time. He advocated a scientific approach based on observation and experiment. To give us an idea of the progression of 17th century English, following is a brief excerpt of his ideas on travel.

Of Travel

Travel, in the younger sort, is part of education, in the elder, a part of
experience. He that traveleth into a country before he hath some entrance
into the language, goeth to school, and not to travel. That young men travel
under some tutor, or grave servant, I allow well; so that he be such a one that
hath the language, and hath been in the country before, whereby he may be
able to tell them what things are worthy to be seen in the country where they
go; what acquaintances they are to seek; what exercises or disciplines the

place yieldeth… (Baugh, 350)

As we can see, the language embodies a view of the times, of how travel should be regarded as well as giving an insight into social class. Its language is close to today's, although some of the wording and structures may be different. For example, the third person singular verb forms of *traveleth, hath, goeth,* and *yieldeth* are now archaic and translate to today's *travels, has, goes,* and *yields*. The word "grave" in "grave servant" may be replaced with *serious*. Indeed, the expression "grave servant" is not something we would use in today's American English, though it does paint a picture of times and circumstances.

In America, early literature coming out of the original colonies carried the expression of British literature of the Renaissance. Writings came to us from John Smith, whose subject matter centered on descriptions of the colonies. After that, much of the literature that followed during this period focused on religious topics, notably Puritanism. Other literature of this period arousing interested involved Indian wars.

The second half of the century embraced the Restoration, with John Dryden the leading figure in England (Baugh 335). Drama, after having taken a downswing for a time, began to become popular again and not just with the elite but with the masses as well. A great variety of poetry was also written during this century, including lyrical as well as heroic or epic verse. Considerable prose was also written, and the term *novel* began to appear. In addition, newspapers and periodicals were published on a regular basis by this time.

Interest in the English language grew. Jonathan Swift and Daniel Defoe were among those to raise that consciousness and express concern over its use and especially over the correct use of the English language.

The 18th Century

Various events shaped the 18th century in England, from Queen Anne's War to a struggle of succession to the English throne. The country was able to develop its economy briefly, until it became involved in a number of other wars, including the Seven Years' War, the American Revolution in 1775, followed by the French Revolution. Many of the problems that brought about these wars continued into the 19th century. The last two of these wars were directly related to a general push for a greater democratic approach to government, although England had little direct involvement in the French Revolution. By then, the Industrial Revolution began to gather momentum with the problems and issues that were to confront the 19th century.

Many great British writers came out of this period. They often dealt with social and political circumstances of the day. A great deal of verse was written during this time, but it was prose that distinguished itself on many topics. Undoubtedly, a significant literary accomplishment was the novel. Among novelists were Jonathan Swift with *Gulliver's Travels*, initially intended as political satire, and Daniel Defoe with *Robinson Crusoe*. In *An Essay on Projects*, Daniel Defoe ponders the status of women. The topic itself is well ahead of its time. On the one hand, it reveals the times in which it was written, while on the other, it foreshadows movements of the 19th and 20th centuries, as the excerpt shows.

An Academy for Women

I have often thought of it as one of the most barbarous customs in
the world, considering us as a civilized and a Christian country, that we
deny the advantages of learning to women. We reproach the sex every day
with folly and impertinence, while I am confident, had they the
advantages of education equal to us, they would be guilty of less than
ourselves. (Baugh, 530)

The language in this selection is so close to today's English that it could almost pass. What gives this page away is the phrase "considering us as a civilized and a Christian country." In the global society of the 21st century, this statement would be politically offense not only in Great Britain but in the United States and other Western countries as well, superseded by the need for racial and economic justice.

The concern over language emanating out of the 17th century resulted in the improvement of dictionaries. English grammars, based on Latin rules began to appear, although at the time, there was no actual awareness of linguistic development. However, the discourse over linguistic rules and usage continued to take place.

In the America of the 18th century, although some religious writing continued, it turned primarily to descriptive writing of the new land. In addition, newspapers and magazines began to appear regularly, becoming very popular. Here, too, the novel made its first attempts. Political writings and essays were also popular. One of the great voices of the time was that of Benjamin Franklin. Following is a brief sample passage from *On Going to Philadelphia,* where Franklin is looking for work as a printer.

Walking again down toward the river, and looking in the
faces of people, I met a young Quaker man, whose

countenance I lik'd, and accosting him, requested he would tell
me where a stranger could get lodging. We were then near the
sign of the Three Mariners. "Here," says he, "is one place that
entertains strangers, but it is not a reputable house; if thee wilt
walk with me, I'll show thee a better." He brought me to the
Crooked Billet in Water Street…. [The next morning]… I made
myself as tidy as I could, and went down to Andrew Bradford
the printer's. (Holmes, 21)

As we can see, the American and British versions of English are very similar. The
object pronoun *thee* is still in use for *you* and so is the now archaic second person
singular form of *wilt* for *will*. The word *countenance*, while it exists in modern English,
would more likely give way to the word *face*. The word *accost* has changed its meaning
to denote a negative act in more recent usage.

In America, much was written both in poetry and prose describing events of the
American Revolution. Undoubtedly, changing the course of history, the most significant and influential piece of writing to emerge from the thirteen original colonies is
The Declaration of Independence signed by the Founding Fathers of what was to become the United States of America. Here is a brief excerpt:

We hold these truths to be self-evident, that all men are
created equal, that they are endowed by their creator with certain
unalienable Rights, that among these are Life, Liberty and the
pursuit of Happiness. That to secure these rights, Governments
are instituted among Men, deriving their just powers from the
consent of the governed, That whenever any Form of Government
becomes destructive of these ends, it is the Right of the People to
foundation on such principles and organizing its powers in such
form, as to them shall seem most likely to effect [sic] their Safety and
Happiness….

Befitting changing times, here was a new way of thinking, a long way from the
divine right of Kings and the supremacy of monarchies. For the first time in the history
of England, voice is granted to those "governed." The language of these carefully chosen words carried their power far into the future on lips of ordinary people.

Because Great Britain was a great power, historically, with its seafaring capabilities, trade and colonization, the influence of the English language eventually drew

larger circles. After the establishment of the United States of America on another continent, English developed its American variation, including pronunciation, usage, idioms, vocabulary, and spelling. Noah Webster began to set forth some of the differences that existed between the languages and published books on spelling and grammar. At the same time, English also began to absorb a great number of words from other languages and other parts of the world: North America contributed such words as *squash* and *moccasin*; Central America contributed *chili* and *coyote;* South America contributed *alpaca, llama, pampas*, and *potato*. India gave us *cashmere, chintz,* and *bungalow*. Africa gave us *chimpanzee* and *zebra*. Australia contributed *boomerang* and *kangaroo*, to name just a few of the many new words entering the English language.

The 19th Century

The 19th century in England brought about a number of movements that grew out of past events in response to economic, political and social circumstances. The greatest influence was the Industrial Revolution which came against the background of the French Revolution and the Napoleonic wars, each with considerable political, economic and social consequences. A major problem soon involved the plight of the laboring classes in relationship to working conditions and hours, child labor, and low wages. While these problems were not immediately solved, humanitarian efforts attempted to deal with them. This resulted in the foundation of hospitals and schools. On the international scene, England's Abolition Movement had the result of abolishing the slave trade. These movements eventually contributed to achieving greater political equality for the middle and lower classes, leading to improved living conditions over time.

Two influences wrought their way through the 19th century. First, Romanticism, having originated in the 18th century, helped shape the literature of the 19th century. It was a reaction against classicism and social convention, a new interest in nature, emotion, and imagination. It came in response, in part, to the French Revolution and the cause of improving and democratizing the political system. Under the Romantics, poetry, prose, the novel, and literary criticism achieved new highs. Poets like William Wordsworth and Samuel Taylor Coleridge, Percy Bysshe Shelly and John Keats made their contributions in England. The novel drew Jane Austen, who wrote about upper middle-class society, such as in *Pride and Prejudice* and Sir Walter Scott, poet and novelist, who focused primarily on historical topics, such as in *Ivanhoe*. Prose found its champions in magazines and periodicals that came into existence, and in newspapers that became more readily available as the general population became more literate.

The second half of the century embraced the Victorian Age in England, a time when Queen Victoria held the throne from 1837-1901. During this time, England started to change from primarily an agricultural nation to an industrial one. Steamships, trains, and telegraphs improved transportation and communication. And despite its internal problems of industrial growth, the country enjoyed stability as a commercial and financial center.

Victorian Writings included a variety of subjects. Scientific advances were being added. One of these was the theory of evolution based on natural selection which Charles Darwin, 1809-1882, discussed in his *Origin of the Species.* Thomas Henry Huxley, 1825-1895, a biologist supporting Darwin's theory, expressed in *Darwiniana* his ideas about scientific process. As we will see, the language used is much like today's, although the type of discussion is characteristic of the 19th century.

> The method of scientific investigation is nothing but the expression of
> the necessary mode of working of the human mind. It is simply the mode
> at which all phenomena are reasoned about, rendered precise and exact….
> In scientific inquiry it becomes a matter of duty to expose a supposed law to
> every possible kind of verification, and to take care, moreover, that this
> is done intentionally, and not left to mere accident…. (Holmes 194)

Victorian writing concerned itself to a great degree with many existing social problems. The plight of workers was seen, chiefly, as a problem attributable to the middle class which many of the writers addressed. In literature, among the poets were Alfred Lord Tennyson and Robert Browning. Prominent novelists included Charles Dickens, Emily and Charlotte Brontë, and George Eliot. Representative writers in specialized fields were, among others, historian Thomas Carlyle and *The French Revolution* and critic John Ruskin and *Modern Painters*, discussing the merits of architecture in *The Stones of Venice.* Many of these ideas still strike a chord in the 21st century, like his two elements of good architecture. The following excerpt will illuminate how the language gradually eased into its late 19th century form.

> The building of the bird and the bee need not express anything like this.
> It is perfect and unchanging. But just because we are something better
> than birds or bees, or building must confess that we have not reached the
> perfection we can imagine, and cannot rest in the condition we have
> attained. If we pretend to have reached either perfection or satisfaction,
> we have degraded ourselves and our work. (Trilling 183)

The language is today's, even if the tone is different. An underlying idea is change. Changing architecture is a part of changing needs, methods, and materials, of changing times, and of progress.

In the United States, the 19th century was a time of great change as well. People were still moving west to settle the country. It was the time of the Gold Rush. The Civil War freed the slaves, and the last of the Indian wars were fought. But, just as in the Old World, railroads and the Industrial Revolution made their way across America.

With much of the country settled, the United States was coming of age and beginning to establish a literary tradition in the sense of the Old World. Essays, poetry, and novels flourished in a variety of areas and voices. Among them was Washington Irving, making his contribution with American legends in *The Sketch Book*, such as "Rip Van Winkle." Novels of James Fennimore Cooper dealt with Western topics in his *Leatherstocking* series. Dealing with social concerns were those of Nathaniel Hawthorne, *The Scarlet Letter*. Mark Twain with *Huckleberry Finn* and *Tom Sawyer* mixed racial disparity with social concern. Herman Melville described the struggle against forces of nature in *Moby-Dick*. Edgar Allan Poe sought out the darker side of life with his stories of horror. Henry James, in *Portrait of a Lady*, rendered a novel about a woman's consciousness and place in the world.

Among poets we find John Greenleaf Whittier and *Snowbound*, Oliver Wendell Holmes and his writings and poetry, and Henry Wadsworth Longfellow, one of the most well-known poets of his time. Yet in the second part of the 19th century two poets started the ball rolling on new ways to perceive and express poetry going forward. Poets representing literary and ideological innovations were Walt Whitman with his open weave style and shocking frankness in *Leaves of Grass* and other poems and Emily Dickinson with her fresh approach and buoyant style in her extensive collection of untitled poems. Dickinson began one of her poems: "This is my letter to the World/ That never wrote to Me – "

The philosophical writings of Ralph Waldo Emerson, including *Nature*, and Henry David Thoreau, including *Walden*, became timeless. In *Walden*, Thoreau philosophizes about language. His ideas are fresh and insightful. He draws a powerful connection between the continuity of history, people, and the development of thoughts and ideas, as we can see from the following excerpt.

… A written word is the choices of relics. It is something at once more intimate with us and more universal than any other work of art. It is the work of art nearest to life itself. It may be translated into every language, and not only be read but actually breathed from all human lips;-- not to be represented on canvas or in marble only, but be carved out of the breath of life itself. The symbol of an ancient man's thought becomes a modern man's speech....

The 19th century wrought its influence on language, continuing to expand and create vocabulary and expressions, adding words, and changing meaning of some existing words. At times, vocabulary originating in different English-speaking countries became shared vocabulary of the English-speaking world. In America, the first lexicographer of consequence was Noah Webster. Having written books on spelling and grammar, he not only studied the differences between British and American English but compiled the first American dictionary. Additions to and improvements and revisions of the dictionary, over time, have served as a model and continue into the 21st century.

The 20th Century

Initially, social, political and economic conditions brought about many changes in 20th century existence, setting the stage for two world wars. World War I was followed by economic depression, widespread unemployment, and social deterioration. These circumstances, then, led to World War II. Both world wars were at the base of political upheavals, economic and social problems, mass destruction, the Holocaust, and great military and civilian casualties. Fortunately, the end of World War II led to economic recovery and industrial growth in the West as well as to a rethinking of ways to resolve international conflict. Nevertheless, World War II was then followed by smaller conflicts and the Iron Curtain, often in the shadow of the struggle between Communism and Democracy.

Warfare had increasingly turned to weapons of mass destruction, made possible by scientific discoveries and industrial advancement. The words *atomic* and *nuclear* were among the most feared in any language of the 20th century. Ironically, with their dual capacity of destruction or benefit the realization over the fact that any people with the right knowledge could develop these powers took hold. Albert Einstein, whose Theory of Relativity revolutionized modern scientific thinking, expressed his concerns over its misuse as well as those of many others in his essay "The Real Problem Is in the Hearts of Men," as the brief excerpt below shows:

…a new type of thinking is essential if mankind is to survive and move to higher levels…. (Holmes 497). All men fear atomic war. All men hope for the benefits from these new powers. Between the realities of man's true

desires and the realities of man's danger, what are the obsolete "realities"
of protocol and military protection? (499)

Other changes were brought about by technological advances and industrial
growth in many areas of existence. World-wide travel by ship, airplane, and automobile
developed and boomed and, along with increasing mass communication, brought the
world closer together. Space exploration led the way to new frontiers, beginning with
the second half of the 20th century. Technology became a way of life, opening doors to
the future. Scientific advances, including those in nuclear physics, not only affected the
way people fought wars but how they lived. Advances in medicine, nutrition, and san-
itation increased life expectancy. And all of these helped expand modern vocabulary.

Urban development and sprawl, particularly in the United States, laying claim to
formerly agricultural lands, was a continuous process in the 20th century and continues
into the 21st. It was an outcome of industrialization and free market economy. Along
with greater development and industrial waste, automobile emissions, use and disposal
of harmful chemicals, such as pesticides and other household and industrial products,
the effects of pollution of land, water, and air are becoming of increasing public concern and often call for political action. In the 20th century, they brought into focus con-
servation groups, such as the Audubon Society, Sierra Club, National Wildlife Feder-
ation, and others, all dedicated to the protection of environment and wildlife in the
United States. The terms *environmental protection* and *global warming* continue to
occupy an important place not only in the U.S. but in Europe and other countries world-
wide as well.

Both Great Britain and the United States experienced many of the same political
events in the 20th century, but some important differences exist. Although affected by
the casualties of foreign wars, including two world wars and other smaller wars through
the 20th century, the U.S., never experienced war with a foreign power on its own soil
up to this time. While Great Britain acquired colonies, the last of which it relinquished
in the 20th century, the United States, historically, preferred to acquire territories close
to its mainland through purchase or by agreement. Eventually, these, such as Louisiana
and Alaska, for example, would be admitted to the Union.

Both countries faced issues on the social front. After a long struggle, women's right
to vote had coined the *suffragette movement.* It had its beginnings in some states of the
U.S. at the end of the 19th century and saw its attainment in other states during the 20th
century. In England, women's right to vote was attained during World War I but in the
U.S. not until 1920. Subsequent to their involvement in the work force during the world

wars, particularly after World War II, women increasingly sought equal rights and equal opportunity.

The 20th century saw the quest of minorities for civil rights, and, in the process, of personal identity and finding of roots, as never before, particularly in the United States. The Civil Rights Movement of the 1960s, led by Dr. Martin Luther King brought about, through peaceful demonstrations, changes on behalf of the Black Community and paved the way for other minority groups as well. The Civil Rights Movement initiated the *multicultural, gender fair, disability sensitive* approach to living and education. Gradually, minorities and women were beginning to step into positions not previously open to them, including in government, elected and appointed. Human rights issues continued to draw attention and to expand throughout the century, including the *gay* "revolution," adding a new meaning to an old, familiar word. And women's struggle for equal opportunity and equal pay for equal work, slow to progress, continue, into the 21st century, while still awaiting passage of the *Equal Rights Amendment.*

Compulsory public education saw its realization in both the United States and Great Britain, increasing literacy of the population. Psychology played an increasing part not only in teaching but, in general, coping with a fast-moving world that seemed to connect as well as disconnect people. New insights contributed meanings to words, such as *conditioning* (Ivan Petrovich Pavlov), *associationism, psychoanalysis* (Sigmund Freud), *numinous, anima, animus, collective unconscious* (Carl Jung), as well as advances in areas like *dyslexia* and *autism.*

Furthermore, in the United States *desegregation* of the public schools became an important issue after the Civil Rights Movement in providing equal opportunity in education for minorities. To this end, public school curriculums were rewritten in Minnesota, like in many other states, to represent the multicultural realities of history, achievement, and culture in textbooks and instruction. *Sexist* and *racist* language lost their ground to *politically correct* expressions to represent the diversity present in the state in particular and in the United States as a whole. Rapidly progressing technological changes and advancements combined with the social changes that developed began to make learning a life-long preoccupation, with graduation from high school or college only the beginning following the new model of continuing education.

Public libraries, having been established in the late 19th and early 20th centuries in Great Britain and in the United States, became an important resource in creating a reading public. Although libraries had their dawn in ancient times, they were not generally accessible to common people, and later, were private collections. Not until the Middle Ages, following the invention of the printing press, did the concept of the modern library find its inception.

Advancements of the century not only improved the literacy rate but made it an absolute necessity not only for an informed citizenry to participate in democratic government, but also to succeed in chosen occupations and professions as well as for the conduct of daily lives. The arts, now more accessible to the general public, flourished in new ways. Writing became increasingly popular as the century progressed, not only because of improved technology but also because of the discovery of the *writing process*. Longer life spans also made increased participation possible. Obviously, many of these events and developments coined their own words and phrases along the way, such as *free writing, e-mail, texting, e-book, key*, and many others.

A variety of literature turned to realism, the effects of national conflicts, social changes and concerns, and eventually also, to the unusual or sensationalistic. In a turning away and rejection of the past, writers exposed what seemed real and unexplored. They availed themselves of new psychological insights and the position of women. War, and particularly recent world wars, revolutions and other political movements and social and racial conditions left their imprint on the literary world in various ways. In the early part of the century, social disillusionment and decay were, also, often at the core. Thus, a new, often free flowing frankness entered the language and subject matter of many subsequent writers with a willingness to avoid social taboos to inform or shock the reader filtered onto the popular scene.

Writing expanded in the 20th century, adding some new genre to what was already written. Poetry was undergoing changes of form and expression. Prose increased in popularity in terms of articles and essays. Fiction and non-fiction were in demand, branching into popular genres of creative non-fiction and memoir. The young adult novel with its brevity made entry and with great success. The novel continued to grow in importance, reflecting movements of the times and changes of society. The genre by now had grown to include not only social concerns, adventure, romance, travel, biography, history, and war but also mystery, horror, fantasy, and science fiction. Informational, scientific, and technical writing, increasingly a necessity, burgeoned as well.

British writers of the early 20th century included the poets William Butler Yeats, American-born T.S. Eliot, and W. H. Auden. Dramatist George Bernard Shaw brought British drama to a new high. Novelists D. H. Lawrence, E.M. Foster, and Thomas Hardy surprised readers with their new frankness and fresh themes. Writers like James Joyce and Virginia Woolf turned to a new style of writing called *stream of consciousness* in an effort to approximate mind processes.

Virginia Woolf in *To the Lighthouse* presents in this characteristic style simultaneously, concerns over the traditional female role and that of the artist, shedding new light on them. She illuminates the creative process as experienced by Lily Briscoe, painting her picture, struggling to find her place in a new vision of a world where women had been expected to play only a supportive role in life. Simple language, rhythmic lines of prose approximating poetry reflect the times in the excerpt below. The word "colour" here is the contemporary British variation of the U. S. spelling of *color*.

> She could have wept. It was bad, it was bad, it was infinitely bad! She could have done it differently of course; the colour could have been thinned and faded; etherealized; that was how Paunceforte would have seen it. But then she did not see it like that…. And it would never be seen; never be hung even, and there was Mr. Tansley whispering in her ear, "Women can't paint, women can't write…" (Woolf 75)

British writer, George Orwell examines problems of colonialism and the rising implications of technology coupled with despotic rule in his work, most prominently *Animal Farm* and *1984*.

American writers of the early 20th century, influenced by some of the same world events as British writers, were influenced predominantly, or course, by American perspectives and circumstances. Novelist Ernest Hemingway's themes reflect revolution and disillusionment in *For Whom the Bell Tolls* and *The Sun Also Rises*. F. Scott Fitzgerald's *The Great Gatsby* embodies both hope and social deterioration. William Faulkner renders the historical South in 20th century perspective of stream of consciousness in *The Sound and the Fury* and *Light in August*. John Steinbeck represents the voice of social protest in *The Grapes of Wrath*. Edith Wharton won a Pulitzer Prize for the novel *The Age of Innocence*. Thornton Wilder won a first Pulitzer Prize with his novel, *The Bridge of San Louis Rey* and a second with his play, *Our Town*.

Poets included T. S. Eliot, *The Love Song of J. Alfred Prufrock*, Ezra Pound, *Cantos*, Edna St. Vincent Millay, *The Harp Weaver*, Carl Sandburg, *Chicago*, Robert Frost, *Poems*, and Langston Hughes, *Selected Poems*. Langston Hughes often applies the spirit of "Roots," as presented in the 20th century TV series of that name which enjoyed great popularity. Hughes reminds us, in his longing, of a roots type of connection in his poem *Sun Song:*

> Sun and softness,
> Sun and the beaten hardness of the earth,
> Sun and the song of all the sun-stars
> Gather together –

Dark ones of Africa,
I bring you my songs
To sing on the Georgia roads.

My soul has grown deep like the rivers. (Hughes 5)

The cultural message of this poem is powerful. He connects existence in a way reminiscent of Thoreau's description of the consummate nature of writing, linking the writer with all that has gone before, making past and present one, or the collective unconscious of Jung, using the phrases "ancient rivers" and "human blood" respectively. In terms of dating language, the word *Negro*, commonly used before the Civil Rights. Movement, has been replaced in usage, including also, such terms as person of color to *Black* and *African American*.

Carl Sandburg captured in his poetry the essence of 20th century mechanization with its self-inflicted, accelerating demands of work out-put, noise and emphasis on speed which, by and by, entered and shaped nearly all areas of living as the century moved forward and still resonates today. The sound of construction with which we live daily echoes in *Good Morning, America:*

The silent litany of workers goes on –
Speed, speed, we are the makers of speed;
Axels, clutches, levers, shovels,
We make the signals and lay the way –
Speed, speed.
The trees come down to our tools.
We carve the wood to the wanted shape
The whining propeller's song in the sky,
The steady drone of the overland truck,
Comes from our hands; us; the makers of speed. (79)

The language Sandburg uses is vivid and three-dimensional in its effect, bringing in the senses, taking us there with its simplicity. This was part of the growing 20th century trend in creative writing and increasingly in other areas of writing as well. The simpler something is said the better, the more concrete, the more accessible it is. The use of bigger, more complex words is increasingly reserved for occasions when nothing else will do. Most of the words in these lines, like *clutch, speed, shovel, shape, whine, song* and others, are of Anglo-Saxon origin. Some of them like *axle, tool* and *sky* come from Old Norse. From Middle English and Old French, derived from Latin, we have *signal, lever,* and *propel. Truck* comes from Latin, derived from Greek.

The second half of the century brought forth a new diversity of writers and topics. Among the writers, Eudora Welty is primarily known for her short stories about America. Kurt Vonnegut, Jr. wrote *Slaughterhouse-Five,* heavily influenced by World War II events.

Increasing numbers of women authors, including minority women, are represented. Joyce Carol Oates, prize-winning author, wrote numerous books, including essays, short stories, poems as well as novels, such as *Poems for Ordinary People.* She advises: "Read widely and without apology. Read what you want to read, not what someone else tells you you should read." Alice Walker won The American Book Award with her novel *The Color Purple.* Ann Tyler's novel, *The Accidental Tourist,* became a movie. Science fiction writer Ursula LeGuin's *The Left Hand of Darkness* won two coveted science fiction awards.

In the world of poetry, Annie Dillard, Adrienne Rich, Gwendolyn Brooks, Anne Sexton, and Maxine Kumin, among many others, became new voices of the century. They represent the rich and unique insight and perspective of these individual women's lives. U.S. Poet Laurate, Billy Collins, discusses the everyday, often with irony or humor, such as in the poem, *Sonnet, w*here he lightheartedly straddles centuries to the present.

The developments, advances, and discoveries in industry, the sciences, and other fields that swept through the 20th century left the English language with a particularly large increase in vocabulary, new uses or meanings added to existing words, as well as many borrowed words. Some words became shortened versions of their originals, such as the word radio from *radiotelegraphy*. Other words, such as *automobile*, derived from Old Greek *auto* + French mobile, came into English in the 19th century, the shortened form of *auto* becoming popular in the 20th century.

Other languages, also, contributed to our word stock in more recent times. For instance, French *télévision* gave English the word *television* which is derived from Greek *tele-*, meaning far, plus *vision*. German gave us such borrowed words, as *gesundheit, angst* (psychology), *blitz* (football), and *blitzkrieg,* among them. Computer science added new meanings to already existing words like, the nouns *menu, mouse, browser, web, home page, app, audio book, touch pad, docking station* among others. Many of them are old familiar words but with new meanings added. Words in the social area include *soccer mom* and *arm candy.* Industry gave us *timeline, day job* and *strip mall*; science gave us *trans fat, hydrogenated vegetable oil.*

The 21st Century

Language continues to expand and change. In 2001, America was rocked by 9/11, the-unthinkable invasion, resulting 2002 in the establishment of Homeland Security. The #MeToo Movement originating 2006, drew wider circles in 2018. Women were elected in record numbers to the House of Representatives in 2018, followed by record numbers of women and minorities putting in their bid for the presidency in 2019. The first woman of color made it into the presidential election as vice president. In 2020, the expression "Black Lives Matter" became front and center, advocating for racial justice. All of these events brought new words and terms into the English language.

Increasingly, industrial and technological innovations affect all areas of life. The internet and social media make large-scale, instantaneous communication the new order of things. In 2004, innovations, such as social media, with Facebook draws billions of users. Space exploration continues with sighting of new planets, activities on the space station, and women becoming part of space crews. Climate change has become a world-wide concern, coining expressions like "global warming" and "climate emergency."

Authors of the 20th century slip into the 21st, while new and diverse voices join the established writers. Literature becomes more profuse than ever, despite or perhaps, because of the changing nature of publication. On the popular scene, people tell their stories in memoir, biography, and creative non-fiction and entertain with popular mystery and romance novels, followed by academic and scientific writing among them.

New Native American voices add perspective with Louise Erdrich, National Book Award winner, author of *The Night Watchman,* a novel based on her grandfather's experience. Alexie Sherman, winner of the National Book Award and other awards, novelist, short story writer, poet, and filmmaker, author of *Face,* has a way to shine a light on indigenous experience, misconceptions and stereotypes, often with humor. He concedes "Humor was an antiseptic that cleansed the deepest wounds."

Conclusion

Modern English exists since approximately 1500. From that time period on considerable vocabulary has been added. Some changes in usage occurred; some words became obsolete or archaic, still others added additional meanings. Minor changes in syntax also occurred. But by and large, the modern reader can easily comprehend the English language from that time period on forward. Affected not only by industrial and technological, economic, social, and multi-cultural advances in the United States, and other western countries of the Indo-European languages, but also by interaction with the global community as well, the English language, always in continuum and development, is what it has become today and will continue to progress thus into the future.

Chapter 9
EVOLUTION OF ENGLISH: OVERVIEW

As we have seen, English, belongs to the Germanic branch of the Indo-European language families. It evolved out of manifold cultural influences and developments of the past, accumulating over the ages a rich language heritage in the process. Old English vocabulary of approximately 50,000-60,000 words has increased to approximately 650,000-750,000 words in Modern English. At the same time, its vocabulary shows a great variety of influences, including Anglo-Saxon, Old Norse, French, Latin, and Greek. The English language can be divided, roughly, into three periods.

The first period, **Old English** dates from approximately 450-1000 A.D., bringing to bear some significant influences. At the outset, Germanic tribes, the Angles, Saxons, and Jutes, invaded the British Isles and imposed their dialects on the Celts living there, with the languages of the Angles and the Saxons eventually becoming most prevalent. An inflected language, it gave English a basic, though small, stock of Germanic vocabulary as well as a Germanic grammatical base. The first stock of vocabulary, thus, came from the Anglo-Saxon and is comprised of simple everyday words that some call "kinship words," like *hand, finger, ring, ball, mother,* and *father*. Among the most often used words in the English language are "and, be, have, it, of, the, to, will," and "you" (Bryant 423), all derived from Anglo-Saxon.

At the same time, the invaders also introduced some Latin, the political and church language of the day. Furthermore, toward the end of this period, the British Isles were invaded again, this time by Norsemen, who added to the newly established language their particular Germanic vocabulary.

The second period, **Middle English**, began, roughly with the Norman Conquest of England in the 11th century, extending to about 1500. The Normans contributed a large French vocabulary to the Germanic base, along with more Latin. Of the established language base, during this time, inflections of words were simplified and grammatical gender was dropped. At the end of the period, the transition from Middle English to Modern English began.

The third period, **Modern English,** dates approximately from 1500. **Early Modern English** began in the 15th century with the Great Vowel Shift, affecting Germanic languages, allowing them to develop each in different directions. For English, this meant the transition from Middle English to Early Modern English. The period extends to about 1700, the age of Shakespeare. **Modern English**, then, dates from about 1700 on to the present. During this time, grammatical changes came about, along with the establishment of formal grammatical rules. More recent modern developments of English primarily concern the expansion and acquisition of new vocabulary.

The **characteristics** that English shares with other Germanic languages, and, therefore, make it a part of the Germanic language family, are as follows:

1. A common vocabulary
2. The verb conjugation system
3. A dental suffix for the past tense
4. Strong and weak adjective declensions
5. A fixed stress accent
6. Vowel changes
7. The First Sound Shift (Algeo 97)

We can trace some of the changes in pronunciation and spelling of Old English (Anglo-Saxon) words as they occurred over these three periods (three nouns and two verbs respectively) on the following chart:

Old English	Middle English	Modern English
gēs	gees	geese
bāt	boot	boat
mūs	mous	mouse
wealcan	walken	walk
habben	haven	have

As we follow the changes of sound and spelling on the list, we can also notice the change of inflection of the verbs walk and have from Old English to Middle English, the inflection being dropped by the time we find it in Modern English.

Words coming from French, Latin, and Greek are usually the more complex words, often relating to government, science, and church. From French we have words like *cousin, infant, flame, declaration,* and *broil*. From Latin come words like *decorum, delinquent, diary,* and *democracy* (derived from Greek). From Greek we have *dialysis, diatheses, stethoscope, thesaurus,* and *thesis* (the last two through Latin).

Words come into existence in a number of ways. First, historically speaking, in the Indo-European languages words are derived from **roots** that exist within the language or language family. Because of the influence of Greek and Latin, many roots originated in these languages. In English most word roots are of Germanic, French, Latin, or Greek origin. To these roots, prefixes and suffixes may be added to form new words with different meanings and functions, each of the languages providing their own characteristic affixes.

Second, words exist in what might be called **word families**. For example, from the Anglo-Saxon word *frēond*, comes the modern word "friend." If we add noun suffixes, we get the words *friendship, friendliness,* and *friendlessness.* Adding other suffixes to the same root word, we get the adjectives *friendly* and *friendless*; adding now a prefix to the adjective, *friendly*, we get another adjective, *unfriendly.* Adding a different prefix to the root word, we get *befriend*, and so on. Although all of these words come from the same root, obviously, they have different meanings and, in many instances, different functions in the sentence.

Similarly, if we look at the word *form*, we find that it comes from the Latin root *fōrma* which became Middle English *forme*, Modern English "form." When we add different prefixes, we have verbs like *inform, conform* and the noun *uniform.* When we add a prefix and a noun suffix to the root word, we have the noun *information*, and if we add another suffix, we have the adjective *informational*, and so on. Another branch of the Latin root *fōrma*, coming into Middle English as *fōrmālis* is the word *formal*, along with its related word group.

Another example is the noun democracy. It comes from the French *dēmocratie*, derived from Latin *dēmokratia* – *dēmos* meaning people and *–kratia*, Latin *–cracy*, meaning government or rule. Different suffixes give us the noun *democrat*, the adjective *democratic*, and the verb *democratize.*

Even today, changing a word's meaning by adding a **prefix or suffix** is still a characteristic of usage and helps make English vocabulary somewhat flexible. However, the original practice of adding a Germanic affix to an Anglo-Saxon word and a Latin affix to a Latin word, may no longer apply respectively in the strictest sense. Affixes today may cross originating languages in English. For example, the word *character* entered the English from the French, derived from the Latin, which derived it from the

Greek *kharaktēr*. When we add the Germanic prefix *un-* and the Greek derived suffixes *–ist* + *-ic*, we have *uncharacteristic*.

Among "living" **suffixes** and **prefixes** still used today to create new words are the following: From Anglo-Saxon, we have the suffixes *–ness, -less,* and *–ish* and the prefix *–un*. From French we have the suffices *–ary, -al, -able,* and *–ous*. From Latin come the suffixes *–tion* and *– ative* and the prefixes *super-, post-,* and *inter-*. From Greek come the suffixes *–ist, -itis,* and *–ize* and the prefixes *anti-, ex-, pro-,* and *hyper-*. Modern words using some of these prefixes, for example, are *hyperactive, postgraduate,* and *Internet* (Bryant 423).

Third, new words are created by **shortening** the original words, such as using *auto* for *automobile, math* for *mathematics* and phone *for* telephone. Similarly, the first letters of names or organizations, groups or other general terms may take the place of the original word. Examples are *UN* for *United Nations, NATO* for *North Atlantic Treaty Organization, PAC* for *Political Action Committee, ESL* for *English as a Second Language, AAUW* for *American Association of University Women.* These new expressions are known as **acronyms.**

Fourth, some words are derived from **names**. Often the name is associated with an invention, innovation or accomplishment by the person or scientist, like *watt, ohm,* and *volt,* or names of philosopher or politician, *Platonic* and *Machiavellian,* for example. Words coming from place names are *hamburger* and *frankfurter,* Hamburg and Frankfurt both cities in Germany.

Fifth, words coined in different English-speaking countries or different areas of the same country called **regionalisms,** have made their own specific contributions to the English-speaking world. Some typically American words are *carpetbagger, charley horse, civil rights, conniption, law-abiding, parlay, semester,* and *sideburns* (Algeo 227).

Among typically British terms are *costermonger, draughts* (game of checkers), and *gangway.* Some words exist in British and American English but with different meanings. With British meanings in parentheses, examples are *boot* (car trunk), *biscuit* (cookie), *underground* (subway), *switchback* (roller coaster), and *holiday* (vacation). Despite regional differences, the English-speaking world has little or no difficulty communicating with each other.

Sixth, **borrowings** from other languages account for about 80% of dictionary entries (Bryant 423). Loan words are words from another language but used in English as its own. Examples of borrowings include words like *sushi* and *samurai* from the Japanese, *hors d'oeuvre, pâté* from French, *schmaltz, schnook, schmooze* from Yiddish, and *angst, Weltanschauung, schnapps, schnauzer* from German. From Native American languages, we have *hickory, igloo, kayak, pecan, squash.*

Seventh, **slang** also creates new vocabulary. Slang is informal language that is used to be original, humorous, create effect, describe a certain group. It often uses figures of speech or short words. Most slang does not remain in the language. This can be evidenced by the expressions peculiar to different generations, such as the expressions *groovy, bad, cool, awesome,* and sweet, all conveying the same meaning, except that each is coined by one generation and generally replaced and discarded by the next.

Over time, many words have **changed sound, spelling**, and **meaning**. For example, *slip* and *glide* became *slide*; *breakfast* and *lunch* became *brunch*. Words like *imp* and *knave*, at one point, simply meant *boy*. The word *free* at one time denoted *noble* or *of high birth* (Bryant 424).

Many recent words coming into the English language since the year 2000 are derived by combining and contracting two existing words into one. Some fun combinations are listed in Merriam Webster's online dictionary like the nouns: *snowpocalypse, thundersnow, greedlock, twirties*; verbs: *ideate, huggle, recombobulate*; adjective: *bipondal.*

Not surprisingly, by 2019, we find continuing changes, additions and mutations of some engrossing words. In the social area we find words, such as the verbs *catastrophizing, defriend* or *unfriend, overthink, and skunked,* the nouns *frenemy, bromance, soft skills, cougar, situatedness*, and *staycation* as well as *peoplekind* and *ancestory*. In technology, we find words like the nouns *paywall, meme, social media, tweet* and the verb *microblog*. In the business world, the nouns *green audit, home-shoring, toxic debt*, and the adjective *overleveraged* are among the entries.

The strengths of English that help make it an international language reside in a number of characteristics. One of these is its wealth of vocabulary accumulated from different sources and the flexibility with which new words are created and continue to enter the language. Areas include a wide range, among them civil rights, science and technology, business and industry, psychology, and popular social trends. Many of our new words are also borrowed by other languages.

Another strength of the English language is its preference for short sentences and a relatively uncomplicated sentence structure and grammar, all of which make it easy to use. Its increasing informality in both speech and writing may also be contributing to its popularity.

Knowledge of another Indo-European language, particularly in the Germanic or Italic language families, along with historical awareness of their influences, is a considerable aid in mastering English spelling.

In addition to an extensive vocabulary, a basic knowledge of language components in addition to its grammar as well as sentence structure take the mystery out of good speech and writing. These allow us to express ourselves with clarity and accuracy in a complex world turning increasingly to writing for creativity, information, exposition, news, communication, and more. Even previously all manual jobs now require adequate language skills with the successful application of technology which has entered nearly every area of employment.

These more specific language skills will be addressed in the following section.

II. COMPONENTS, STRUCTURES, AND PRINCIPLES OF ENGLISH:

There is properly no history; only biography.
~Ralph Waldo Emmerson

I hear America singing ….
~Walt Whitman

What the finger writes the soul can read.
~Alice Waler

The Fog comes on little cat feet.

~ Carl Sandburg

So it was like that, James thought,
the lighthouse one had seen across
the bay all these years.
~Virginia Woolf

On the Apollo moon landing: "That's one small step
for man, one giant leap for mankind."
~Neil Armstrong

You can't use up creativity.
The more you use, the more you have.
~Maya Angelou

The more developed and extensive a person's language skills the better he or she will be able to communicate with others, whether at home, with friends, or in the workplace.

A. Sentence Components:
Parts of Speech

Principles connect component parts of speech, to create sentences that lead to the field of writing.

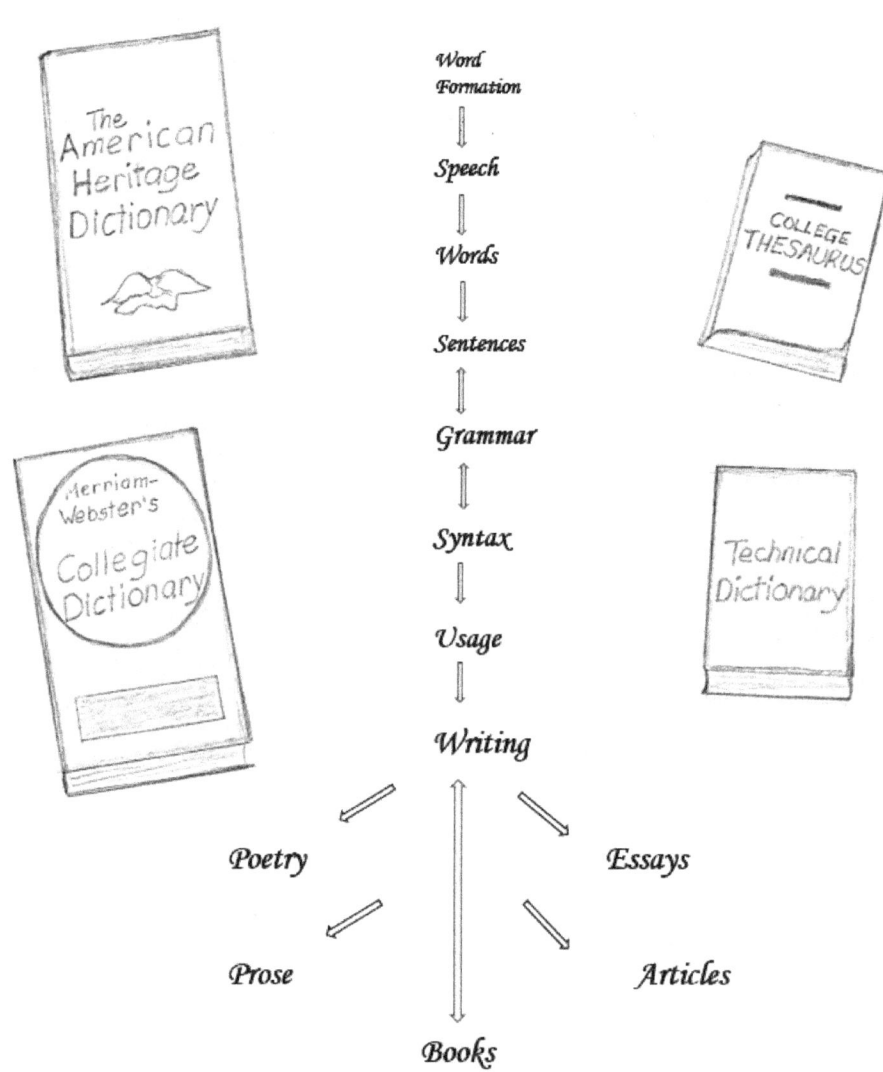

Introduction: Solving the Puzzle of English

In our daily speech we are used to draw from what seems an inexhaustible well of words. We tend to communicate spontaneously as the need arises without too much thought how to formulate sentences. We are on a kind of automatic pilot, influenced by the type of language we are used to speak and hear around us. We say what we want to say, accompanied by gestures that punctuate our meaning. When we misspeak or do not make ourselves clear, we can correct what we say, or our conversational partner can ask questions.

But once we sit down to write, the well of ideas and words may easily overwhelm us with its flow, and our task of writing may transform into a puzzle. We may not only be plagued by what we want to say and how to say it but, also, by how to put it in writing.

Since we have to rely on structures and punctuation to separate and represent thought units, without gestures, voice inflections, or chance to answer questions, this section will help us understand the parts of speech that construct these thought units which become the components of our sentences. These will be discussed under sentence types. As writers, it helps us acknowledge that language, by means of its blueprint called grammar, is an area of expertise just like the sciences, trades, businesses, or the arts, all require knowledge and skill in their application.

The discussion of parts of speech here is an updated, user-friendly approach designed to meet the needs of today's writers of all ages. It aims to reveal grammatical relationships, without shortcuts, minimizing, or tedious exercises. The idea is not only to recognize words and word forms but to understand how and when to use them. To this end, a combination of functional and traditional grammar help to take the guess work out of identifying parts of speech and give users a better understanding of word function and language patterns. Particular attention is given to verb conjugation of both regular and irregular verbs and their uses. An appendix of irregular verbs is included in the book. This approach is also helpful in preparation for second language study.

While this section will be particularly helpful to beginners, those who already have a background in grammar will find it convenient on those occasions when they need to verify or ascertain some specific points of grammar. *Power Behind Your Writing: What Every Writer Needs to Know*, by exposing the essentials of language and writing, serves as a handy reference and should be part of a writer's tool kit, just like a good dictionary and thesaurus.

Chapter 10
NOUNS ARE STARTERS

THE NEW GAME

Name the game.
Kick off the play.
Follow the players
passing the ball.

Watch the people
in the stands
ride the action
shouts and jeers
boos and cheers,
goals into their dreams.

Nouns are the most basic words in our language. They are among the first words a small child learns, because they name things. As a matter of fact, the word *noun* comes from the Latin word *nomen,* meaning *name.*

Nouns Can Be Identified in Various Ways

1. Most popularly, in **traditional grammar** a **noun is** defined as **a word that names a person, animal, place, thing or idea**, for example: *boy, tiger, city, book, and   decision.*

2. When we look at a noun in **functional terms**, we discover that **all nouns** can be **preceded by articles.** Nouns can be preceded by the **definite article,** *the* or by the **indefinite articles,** *a or an*. Use *an* before nouns that begin with a vowel, *a* before nouns that begin with a consonant. **Before a plural noun use some.** These little words can be used as noun identifiers when we want to test if a word is used as a noun.

For example –

singular:	the apple	a house	an owl
plural:	the baskets	some children	some books

3. Another way to recognize many nouns is by their **endings or suffixes**. Among common noun suffixes are *-tion, -sion, -ance, -ence, -ment, -ness, -cy, -ia, -ity, -age*.

-tion	**-sion**	**-ance**	**-ence**
attention	decision	assurance	dependence
determination	revision	insurance	difference
education	incision	attendance	presence

-ment	**-cy**	**-ia**	**-ity**
employment	bankruptcy	anemia	possibility
enjoyment	democracy	encyclopedia	activity
advertisement	intricacy	Bolivia	sensibility

-age	**-ness**
blockage	gentleness
breakage	happiness
adage	kindness

Nouns referring to people or actions often end in *–er* or *–or*. The suffix *-or* can also point to specific behavior, state or quality.

-er		**-or**	
player	boiler	inspector	color
banker	trailer	projector	glamor
interpreter	planter	inventor	honor

4. Another characteristic of nouns is that they can add **plural endings**. This holds true for the majority of English nouns. Here are some common plural endings.

a. Most English nouns add an **–s** to form their plural.

    students   monkeys

    trees   banjos

    sons   pianos

    boys

b. Some nouns add **–es** if the plural *–s* alone cannot be sounded out.

    churches   kisses   quizzes

    bridges   bushes

    buses   axes

    Some nouns ending in *o* add **–es**.

    echoes   heroes   potatoes

c. Nouns that end in *y*, preceded by a consonant, change the *y* to *I* and add **–es**. Thus, you have:

    city > cities   body > bodies   cry > cries

d. Some nouns keep the same form in the plural, particularly those referring to animals.

    sheep   deer   fish

e. Some Greek – Latin derived words still use their Latin or Greek endings, even though the Anglicized plural has been added more recently. Dictionaries list the preferred version first.

    syllabus, -buses or –bi   crisis, crises

    cactus, -ti or –tuses   basis, bases

    stimulus, -li   neurosis, neuroses

    oasis, oases   medium, -dia or –diums

    curriculum, -lums or –la   stadium, -diums or –dia

f. Collective nouns are usually singular in form and do not end in "s." Collective nouns generally represent a group. This group can describe people or ideas, animals, or things.

Collective Nouns

navy	police
team	class

> For example: The **army** fought off the invaders.

The collective noun *army* is singular, even though it represents a group. The noun *invaders* is plural and, therefore, carries an "s" ending; it is not a collective noun.

Nouns Can Be Divided into Two Categories: Concrete and Abstract

Concrete nouns refer to real experience. In other words, these are things we can experience through the senses. We can see, hear, smell or touch them. Abstract nouns, on the other hand, have primarily a meaning of idea. They may have different intended meanings, depending on the situation or the speaker. Most abstract nouns cannot be experienced by the senses.

Concrete Nouns	Abstract Nouns
boy	liberty
woman	democracy
panther	tyranny
robin	thought
North America	greatness
Europe	love
bridge	hate
window	happiness
pencil	disaster
key	behavior
ball	meaning

Proper Nouns

Proper nouns are like other nouns in that they name someone or something. But they refer to a specific person, place, animal, organization, idea or thing. For this reason, proper nouns are capitalized.

Proper Nouns		Common Nouns
Monday (days of	Mallory (name)	girl
the week)	Mr. Jones	coach

January (months)	Vikings	team
Asia (continent)	National League	football
Mars	President Washington	president
Wisconsin	(title)	school
Minneapolis	White House	house
West High School	American Revolution	revolution
Jaguar (name of a car)		

Nouns are important, because they fulfill different functions in a sentence, as we will see later when we discuss parts of the sentence. When they are the subject, they initiate action. When they are the object, they receive the action of the verb. Sometimes they may even be the object of a preposition.

In summary, as we have seen, nouns can be recognized in many different ways: by definition, by their function, their endings, their capacity to form plurals. Being familiar with these features will not only help us recognize nouns more easily, but they will help make us aware of the way some nouns are formed. This, in turn, will help us with our spelling. What a bonus!

Exploring Language

1. In the poem at the beginning of the chapter, find the nouns and identify them in the various ways outlined in this chapter.

2. Write your own noun poem or paragraph.

3. Or, write a poem or paragraph about a single noun of your choice. Write its story, the story of what it means to you. How have you experienced its life?

4. Write down the definition of a favorite or selected noun. Look up its word history. Then look up its cultural meaning or development in an encyclopedia. You may want to write a brief report, including your conclusions on your findings.

Chapter 11
PRONOUNS ARE STAND-INS

OUR GAME

They play the game;
we watch their moves.
We sing our song of cheer,
throw ourselves
into the quest,
their play – our hope,
their win – our triumph!

Pronouns often take the place of nouns. The word pronoun is made up of the prefix *pro-* plus the word *noun*. *Pro-* comes from Latin and means *for*. They help us avoid repetition and can give us another reference to the subject or object, such as gender, number, etc. Various kinds of pronouns exist, depending on the function and use they have in the sentence. Knowing when to use the appropriate pronoun is easy once you have learned their function.

Personal Pronouns

Personal pronouns usually refer to a specific person or thing. They can be divided into **object pronouns** and **subject pronouns.** Knowing the order in which the "persons" are arranged will help us remember the groupings. Keeping the groupings separate will help us use the pronouns correctly in a sentence. The bonus here is, when we study a second language, understanding these sequences is also extremely helpful.

		Subject Pronouns		Object Pronouns
	>	1st person	I	me
Singular	>	2nd person	you	you
	>	3rd person	he, she, it	him, her, it
	>	1st person	we	us
Plural	>	2nd person	you	you
	>	3rd person	they	them

Subject pronouns always take the place of the subject in the sentence.
Example:

1. **I** saw his friends at the ball game. *I* is the subject pronoun.

2. **You** and **I** went to the ball game together. *You* and *I* are compound subjects.

3. **They** played a good game. *They* is the subject pronoun.

   A Note about Usage: In spoken language particularly, it is common for some people to use object pronouns instead of subject pronouns. This substitution has become quite common. For example:

Incorrect: Him and me went to the store.   **Correct:** He and I went to the store.

The pronouns *him* and *me* in the incorrect example are object pronouns used in place of subject pronouns.

Incorrect: She is bigger than me.   **Correct:** She is bigger than I.

   Note: Although the use of *me* in the following statement, "She is bigger than me," is increasingly used in informal or spoken English, in more formal English, the subject pronoun "I" should follow, since the verb *be* is also a linking verb. Linking verbs do not take direct objects but are followed in the predicate by the nominative case which is the subject, as shown in the example above. Therefore, the verb *be* is followed in traditional or formal English by a subject pronoun.

Object pronouns, as the name suggests, take the position of the object in the sentence.
 Example:
1. The spectators watched **him** score. The spectators are the subject. *Him* is the direct object of the verb *watched*.

2. Heidi saw him at the game. *Heidi* is the subject; *him* is the direct object of the verb *saw*; *game* is object of the preposition *at*.

3. **We** spoke English to **them.** *We* is the subject pronoun; *English* is the direct object; *them* is object of the preposition *to*.

4. Scott saved a cookie for **her** and **me.** *Scott* is subject. *Cookie* is object of *saved*. *Her* and *me* are compound objects of the preposition *for*.

   Note: If prepositions are followed by a pronoun or pronouns, they are generally object pronouns.

Reflexive Pronouns
Reflexive pronouns always refer back to the subject.

		Reflexive Pronouns	
	>	1st person	myself
Singular	>	2nd person	yourself
	>	3rd person	himself, herself, itself
	>	1st person	ourselves
Plural	>	2nd person	yourselves
	>	3rd person	themselves

Example:
Her little brother washed **himself** for the first time. *Himself* is used reflexively, because it refers back to the subject, *her little brother*.

Possessive Pronouns

Possessive pronouns are also called possessive adjectives. They are pronouns because they have "person" categories. They are adjectives, because they usually precede nouns. Other possessive pronouns may be used with the verb *to be*.

			Used with Noun	**Used with Verb**
	>	1st person	my	mine
Singular	>	2nd person	your	yours
	>	3rd person	his, her, its	his, hers, its
	>	1st person	our	ours
Plural	>	2nd person	your	yours
	>	3rd person	their	theirs

Examples:

1. My book is on the table. *My* tells whose book it is. *Book* is a noun. *My book* is the subject in the sentence.

2. The students are telling **their** stories. *Their* tells whose stories they are. Stories is a plural noun. *Their stories* is the object in the sentence.

3. The pen is **mine**. *Mine* tells to whom the pen belongs. It follows the verb *is*.

4. The footballs are **theirs**. *Theirs* tells to whom the footballs belong. *Theirs* follows the verb *are*.

Interrogative Pronouns

Interrogative pronouns are question words. These words ask about people or things. They are:

who   whom   whose   which   what

Examples:

1. **Who** is the new student in class?

2. The lecturer, **who** passed out the notes, speaks to the audience.

3. The man, to **whom** we presented the award, is not here today.

4. To **whom** does this pencil belong?

5. **Which** one of the reports is yours?

6. **What** did you have for lunch today?

A Note about Usage: The use of the pronouns *who* and *whom* depends on their function in the sentence. *Who* is used as *subject* or in *nominative* position and *whom* is used in *object* position. In example 1 *who* is the subject in the sentence. In example 2 *who* refers back to the subject, *the man*. In example 3 *whom* is object of the verb *present*, and in example 4 it is object following the preposition *to*. However, the use of *whom* is rare in speech and informal writing today, because it is considered too formal or stilted.

Demonstrative Pronouns

Demonstrative pronouns point out things or people. Demonstrative pronouns are:

| this | that | these | those |

This and *these* point things out close to the speaker. *That* and *those* point things out farther in the distance.

Examples:

1. **This** book is a mystery.

2. **That** one is a biography.

3. **These** books are for my students.

4. **Those** books belong to another class.

Indefinite Pronouns

Indefinite pronouns take the place of nouns that are general. They are somewhat more difficult to identify than other pronouns. The following are pronouns that take the place of singular nouns:

any	each	everybody	somebody	either
anyone	one	everyone	someone	neither
anybody	no one	everything	something	nothing
anything	nobody			
another				

The following **indefinite pronouns** are plural:

both	few	many	several

The next group of **indefinite pronouns** can be either singular or plural:

all	none	some

Examples:

1. **No one** could answer the question.

2. **Something** was making a noise outside.

3. The lunch menu had **nothing** he liked.

4. **Few** could make it to the finish line.

5. **Some** like hot peppers.

6. **All** joined in the song.

In summary, the English language has several different groups of pronouns. Each group has a specific use. The most commonly used pronouns, subject and object pronouns, have each a distinct function but are the ones most easily confused and therefore transposed, particularly in spoken English. Knowing how to use pronouns correctly helps us express ourselves more accurately. So, go ahead, spread the word about pronouns. You could lead the way!

Exploring Language

1. Find the pronouns in the poem at the beginning of the chapter and identify them according to the various ways outlined.

2. Write your own poem or a brief essay and see how many pronouns you have included in order to avoid repetition.

3. Write an essay or a poem about the pronoun *I*. Let yourself write for about five or ten minutes non-stop. See what you will discover.

Chapter 12
ADJECTIVES COLOR NOUNS

PASSAGE

Eager mind,
difficult move,
playful spirit,
determine the game

in the field of dreams.

Players catch the fast ball,
lose the curve ball,
hope and train,
play and work

in the maze of life.

Seeking fun,
we find our sport in life.
A game well played
becomes its own reward
in the final call.

Adjectives can make our language more vivid and exact. The word *adjective* comes from the Latin *adjicere*, meaning to add to. As we have seen, nouns name something. Adjectives describe that something or someone, namely the noun, further.

Adjectives Describe Nouns

Adjectives describe nouns by telling: **How many? Which one? What kind?** They usually precede the noun.

Examples:

Five people entered the auditorium together. *Five* describes the noun by telling how many people.

The **tall** man is the **younger** brother. *Tall* and *younger* tell which one.

They served a **cold** meal at the meeting. *Cold* tells which kind.

Sometimes, more than one adjective may be desirable. In this case, we often separate the adjectives by placing a comma between them.

Examples:

His **older, wiser, more experienced** brother showed him the ropes.

If the first adjective describes the entire phrase, the comma may be omitted after the first adjective, depending on the emphasis.

Examples:

Ginny wears the **new red** dress.

She drives an **expensive old** car.

Many Adjectives Can Be Recognized by Their Form

While many adjectives, like warm, great, sad, have no ending in common, many other adjectives do. They are often formed by adding a specific suffix to a noun or verb. This is one area where we can still be creative with the English language – forming our own adjectives. Consider the following listing.

-able	-al	-ant	-ed
adorable	horizontal	defiant	fascinated
capable	intentional	expectant	interested
lovable	monumental	reluctant	opinionated

-ent	-escent	-ese	-ful
absorbent	adolescent	Japanese	joyful
dependent	effervescent	Chinese	playful
benevolent	juvenescent	Vietnamese	tearful

-ish	-less	-like	-ous
childish	clueless	childlike	hideous
fiendish	helpless	masklike	ominous
stylish	homeless	godlike	porous

-y
hungry
stocky
stormy

Adjectives Can Be Compared

The comparison of adjectives expresses
greater degree between the quality of two or more items. The superlative indicates
the greatest degree of quality between three or more things or people.

Examples:

Jeff is tall.   Scott is taller.   Dan is tallest.

1. Most adjectives of one syllable and some of two syllables add an **–er** ending to
   form the comparative and an **–est** ending to form the superlative. Here is what
   they look like:

Positive	Comparative	Superlative
bold	bolder	boldest
fine	finer	finest
great	greater	greatest
long	longer	longest
nice	nicer	nicest
old	older	oldest
short	shorter	shortest
young	younger	youngest

2. When a single consonant follows a short vowel at the end of the adjective, the consonant doubles to preserve the sound.

hot	hotter	hottest
fat	fatter	fattest

3. When an adjective ends in *y*, the *y* will change to *i* before adding **–er** in the comparative and **–est** in the superlative.

dry	drier	driest
early	earlier	earliest
happy	happier	happiest
heavy	heavier	heaviest
lovely	lovelier	loveliest
tasty	tastier	tastiest

4. The words **more** and **most** are used for many adjectives of two syllables and for all adjectives of three syllables or more.

balanced	more balanced	most balanced
colorful	more colorful	most colorful
distinguished	more distinguished	most distinguished
fantastic	more fantastic	most fantastic
urgent	more urgent	most urgent

5. Some adjectives are irregular when they change form in their comparative and superlative degrees.

bad	worse	worst
good	better	best
much	more	most

Proper Adjectives

Proper adjectives are capitalized. Proper adjectives are formed from proper nouns.

Examples:

> 1. **American** students carried their books.
> 2. The robot moved across **Martian** terrain.
> 3. They liked the **Asian** restaurant.

Other Words Used as Adjectives

Words, such as nouns and certain pronouns, can also be used as adjectives.

1. **Possessive pronouns generally serve as adjectives** in the sentence. They, too, precede the noun. They may also precede other adjectives. There is no comma between the possessive adjective and the adjective it p cedes.

Examples:

My brother got a new bicycle.

Our second dishwasher broke down yesterday.

His new, green sweater is in the wash.

2. **Nouns are sometimes used as adjectives**, when they precede other nouns.

Examples:

The **track** meet started early in the season. *Track* is a noun serving as an adjective describing the noun, *meet*.

The **baseball** mitt got a good workout this time around. *Baseball* is a compound noun serving as an adjective describing the noun, *mitt*.

He put the **new bicycle** wheels in the **old tool** shed. *New* is an adjective; *bicycle* is a noun used as an adjective; *new* and *bicycle* describe the noun, wheels. *Old* is an adjective; *tool* is a noun used as an adjective; both describe the noun, *shed*.

Adjectives Follow Linking Verbs

Linking verbs are verbs like *be, become, appear, remain, grow, stay* and include verbs of the senses, such as *feel, look, smell, sound, taste.*

Examples:

The **candy** bar tastes **good**. *Candy* is a noun used as an adjective; *good* is an adjective following the linking verb, *tastes*.

The students appeared **happy** after **their** trip. *Happy* is an adjective following the linking verb, *appeared*; *their* is a possessive adjective preceding the noun, *trip*.

After **nine** hours of travel, I feel **tired**. *Nine* is an adjective preceding the noun, *hours*; *tired* is an adjective following the linking verb, *feel*.

Adjectival Forms Can Function as Nouns

Sometimes adjectival forms can also function as nouns.

Examples:

He presented the report for the **good** of the community. *Good* is used here as a noun, preceded by the definite article, *the,* the noun indicator.

He walked through the **thick** of it. *Thick* is an adjective used here as a noun, preceded by the definite article.

As we have seen, adjectives describe nouns by telling something specific about them. Adjectives can often be recognized by their endings. They can compare quality. Proper adjectives are capitalized. Sometimes nouns and possessive pronouns can function as adjectives. Other times adjectives can function as nouns. Adjectives can also follow linking verbs. Adjectives let us add detail and interest to our writing. But, adjectives should be used sparingly in writing, if possible. Now go ahead, color your language with care!

Exploring Language

1. In the poem at the beginning of the chapter, find the adjectives.

2. Write a short poem or a paragraph about a sport or leisure time activity. Then check for adjectives. Did you have many? What happens when we use adjectives too frequently? You may want to experiment here.

3. Think of an interesting adjective. Write a paragraph or two about it. Let it take you wherever it wants to go. What did you discover in the process?

Chapter 13
VERBS MOVE BODY AND MIND

THE BAND

I play the guitar.
You play the keyboard.
He beats the drums.
She sings the song.

It's fun to play in a band.

We enter the stage
and greet the audience.
They are the fans,
who cheer us on.

Verbs help us communicate what the subject is doing, thinking, feeling or what state it is in. The term *verb* comes from the Latin *verbum*, meaning word. Verbs show person, number, tense, voice and mood. The verb is the second basic element needed to form a sentence.

For example
Students **are writing** reports.   *Students* is the subject; *are writing* are the verbs (verbal phrase). Reports is the direct object.

We **ate** pie after the movie.   *We* is the subject pronoun; *ate* is the verb; *after the movie* is the prepositional phrase.

The baby **will sleep** all afternoon. *The baby* is the subject; *will sleep* is the verbal phrase; *all afternoon* is the adverbial phrase telling when.

Types of Verbs

1. **Most verbs** fall into three categories:

Physical Action	Mental Action	State of Being
walk	think	stand
talk	dream	sit
play	sense	hold

2. **Linking verbs.** These are verbs of the senses. They link the subject with another word in the sentence. Linking verbs differ from other verbs in that they are followed by adjectives, instead of adverbs, called predicate adjectives or predicate nouns.

be (and all its forms)	feel	remain	sound
appear	grow	seem	stay
become	look	smell	taste

Examples:

Dan **became** a doctor. *Dan* is the subject; the verb *became* links *Dan* with *doctor*.

The snow **was** deep. *The snow* is the subject; w*as* is the verb linking the adjective *deep* with *snow*.

3. **Helping or auxiliary verbs.**
   a. The most common **helping verbs**, also called auxiliary verbs, are *be, do, have*. We use these primarily to indicate tense or duration. Their infinitives are:

to be	to have	to do

Here are some sentence **examples**:

John **is writing** a letter to Susan.

John is the subject; *is* is the helping verb for the main verb, *writing*.

I **have been throwing** the ball into the net.

I is the subject; *have been* are helping

verbs for the main verb, *throwing*.

Jeff **did throw** the ball that broke the window.

Jeff is the subject; *did* is the helping
verb for the main verb, *throw*. *Broke* is a verb.

Sometimes **helping verbs** also function **as main verbs** in a sentence.

Examples:

His little brother **is** five years old.

His little brother is the subject; *is* is the main verb.

Scott **has** the money for the movies.

Scott is the subject; *has* is the main verb.

b. **Modal Auxiliaries** are **another type of helping verb**. They can express mood or tense and are used with the infinitive of the main verb. The verb, *will,* is generally used with the infinitive of the main verb to express future tense.

Modal Auxiliaries

can	must	shall	will
may	ought	should	would

Verb Conjugation and Tense

Verbs show both conjugation and tense. This is, by the way, another simple way in which we can identify verbs. **Verb conjugation** occurs when the verb form agrees with the person to which it is linked. The unchanged or base form of the verb is called the **infinitive.** In English, the infinitive is preceded by **to,** although the dictionary does not list verbs that way. For example, the infinitive form of **think** is *to think*; the infinitive form of **come** is *to come*, etc. Knowing this helps, also, in second language learning.

All verbs can be conjugated. This means showing the varying verb forms for the different persons, singular and plural. We are using the conjugated form of the verb **to walk,** when we say *he walks. Walks* is the form of the verb we use to agree with *he.* Although in the English language, there remains primarily the -*s* ending for the third person singular in the present tense, we are confronted with changes in conjugational form in an irregular verb like *to be*, as we shall see. Knowing how conjugation works helps us grasp the fact that verbs can change their forms or spelling, as the verb, *be,* does and as other irregular verbs do. It also helps us in learning a second language, particularly one belonging to the Indo-European family of languages, where these changes in form for different persons generally do occur.

1. **The Present Tense.** The present tense describes action taking place today, right now. There are three ways to express tense: First, with the form of the verb, present tense; second, with the helping verb *be* and the present participle, progressive tense; third, with a form of *do* and main the verb, emphatic mode. Each of these forms, however, may convey a slightly different meaning. The following chart shows **present tense conjugation**:

Present Tense Verb Conjugation

infinitive:	**to walk**	**Present**	**Progressive**	**Emphatic**
	1st person	I walk	am walking	do walk
singular>	2nd person	you walk	are walking	do walk
	3rd person	he, she, it walks	is walking	does walk
	1st person	we walk	are walking	do walk
plural>	2nd person	you walk		
	3rd person	they walk		

Sentence **examples**:

The student **reads** the book.

Reads is present tense, third person singular of the verb *to read.*

We **ride** to school on the bus.

Ride is present tense, first person plural.

He **is going** to work early every morning.

The helping verb *is* is used with the present participle, *going*, to express continuous action taking place in the present. This verb combination is called the present progressive.

John **does know** the answer.

The helping verb *does* emphasizes that John, indeed, *knows* the answer.

The helping verbs. The verb *to be* also functions as a helping verb. It is an irregular verb. That means it does not follow the normal conjugation pattern the way the regular verb *walk* does. The conjugational forms keep changing for first, second, and third persons singular, with all three plural persons the same as the second person singular.

infinitive: **to be**					
	1st person	I **am**		1st person	we **are**
singular>	2nd person	you **are**	plural>	2nd person	you **are**
	3rd person	he, she, it **is**		3rd person	they **are**

The verb *to have* also functions as a helping verb and is also an irregular verb, although in the present tense, it shows only one irregular form, namely the third person singular.

infinitive: **to have**					
	1st person	I have		1st person	we have
singular>	2nd person	you have	plural>	2nd person	you have
	3rd person	he, she, it **has**		3rd person	they have

Like the verb *have,* the conjugation of the helping verb *do*, stays the same for all persons, except third person singular, where it changes to *does*.

2. The Past Tense. The past tense describes action that took place in the past.

a. Regular verbs form their past tense by adding *–ed* to the stem of the verb for all persons, singular and plural.

Past Tense of Regular Verbs

infinitive: **to dance**		Past	Progressive	Emphatic
singular>	1st person	I danced	was dancing	did dance
	2nd person	you danced	were dancing	
	3rd person	he, she, it danced	was dancing	
plural>	1st person	we danced	were dancing	
	2nd person	you danced		
	3rd person	they danced		

b. Irregular verbs. Irregular verbs generally do not add the *-ed* ending to the stem of the verb in the past tense. Instead, they may form their past tense with a vowel change, sometimes, with a change in spelling, or a form that looks like a different word altogether, such as *go* changing to *went*.

Past Tense of Irregular Verbs

infinitive: **to drive**		Past	Progressive	Emphatic
singular>	1st person	I drove	was driving	did drive
	2nd person	you drove	were driving	
	3rd person	he, she, it drove	was driving	
plural>	1st person	we drove	were driving	
	2nd person	you drove		
	3rd person	they drove		

Sentence **examples**:

1. John **drove** the car to the banquet hall.

2. Our family **was driving** on I-94, when we **spotted** the hot air balloon.

3. His mother **made** sure that he **did drive** his sister to volleyball practice.

All three sentences above express action in the past, but each sentence has a slightly different emphasis. Sentence number 1 simply expresses past action. Sentence number two, *was driving,* expresses the progressive past, showing continuity of action, when something else, *spotted...,* took place. In sentence number three, *made* expresses the simple past, while the helping verb, *did,* emphasizes the main verb, *drive.*

The helping verbs *have* and *be* are among the irregular verbs. The verb *have* changes to *had* for all persons, singular and plural in the past tense. But the verb *be* changes to *was* in the first person singular and to *were* for the remaining persons, singular and plural. The verb *do* changes to *did* for all persons, singular and plural.

3. **The Present Perfect Tense.** This tense refers to action that has been completed. It requires the present tense of the helping verb *have* plus the past participle of the main verb. For action that has been continuous, we need the helping verb, *have*, plus the past participle of *be* (*been*), plus the present participle of the main verb.

Examples:

> The students **have read** the books.
> The women **have been working** on the report all day.

4. **The Past Perfect Tense.** The past perfect tense refers to action that took place in the past before something else happened in the past. To form the past perfect tense requires the helping verb *have* plus the past participle of the main verb. For the progressive, action that shows continuity, we need the past tense of the helping verb, plus the past participle of *be* (*been*) plus the past participle of the main verb, in a construction similar to the present perfect tense. **Examples**:

> He **had asked** for permission to use his father's car, before he left.
> They **had been driving** a long time, when they came to the lake.

5. **Principal Parts of Regular Verbs.** The principal parts of verbs are: the infinitive; the third person singular, past tense; the present participle; and the past participle. When verbs are regular, these are easy to remember, because the stem of the verb adds *-ed* in the past tense, *-ing* for the present participle, and *-ed* for the past participle, the same as for the past tense. See the chart below.

Principal Parts of Regular Verb

Infinitive	Past Tense	Present Participle	Past Participle
walk	walked	walking	walked
dance	danced	dancing	danced
hope	hoped	hoping	hoped

A note about **verbs ending in –*ie* and –*y*.** Verbs ending in –*ie* generally form their past tense and past participle by simply adding a –*d*. Thus, *tie* becomes *tied, lie* becomes *lied*. The present participle changes the –*ie* to –*y*, thus *tying* and *lying*.

Most verbs ending in –*y* change to –*ie* before adding the –*d* in the past tense but retain their –*y* ending before adding the –*ing* to form the present participle.

Infinitve	Past Tense	Present Participle	Past Participle
apply	applied	applying	applied
deny	denied	denying	denied
hurry	hurried	hurrying	hurried

6. **Principal Parts of Irregular Verbs.** Irregular verbs do not usually add -*ed* to the stem of the verb to form the past tense. Instead, their past tense is often formed by changing the vowel of the verb root. Sometimes, the change in the past tense is so extreme that it appears like a different word altogether, as in the verb *go*, for example, which changes to *went* for all persons, singular and plural. While the present participle of irregular verbs is also formed the by adding -*ing* to the root of the verb, the past participle, on the other hand, may carry a vowel change and end in -*d*, -*e*, -*g*, -*en*, -*n*, or –*t* most frequently, for example. While some of the verbs are part of a pattern, changes are often unpredictable. That is why it is helpful to memorize the principal parts of irregular verbs (see Appendix, Irregular Verbs Chart, where they have been grouped according to conjugational similarities).

Some irregular verbs retain the form of the base verb (root) in the past tense and past participle, among them *cut, hit, put, quit, read, shut, spit.* Verbs ending in –*d or –t* preceded by a short vowel sound in the infinitive will double that consonant to form the present participle.

Infinitive	Past	Present Participle	Past Participle
cut	cut	cutting	cut
but:			
read	read	reading	read

7. **The Future Tense.** The future tense refers to action that will happen in the future. It can be expressed in one of three ways. First, the future tense is formed by using the helping verb *will* in combination with the main verb. Second, it also uses the progressive and, third, the emphatic using the present participle *going.*

---

infinitive: to walk

	future	progressive	emphatic
sing.>	I will walk		
	you will walk		
	he, she, it will walk	she will be walking	it is going to walk
pl.>	we will walk		
	you will walk		
	they will walk		

Example: The student **will ask** the teacher for the information.

When we describe **progressive action** in the future tense, for example, we use *will* in combination with the helping verb *be* and *the present participle of the main verb.*

Example: Some of her friends **will be bringing** guests to the meeting.

We express future action, in spoken language particularly, by using the verb *go* in combination with a form of *be*, plus the *infinitive of the main verb.*

Example: I **am going to see** him on Saturday.

8. **The Future Perfect Tense.** This tense indicates action that will be completed sometime in the future. It uses *will have* in combination with the past participle of the main verb.

Example: | Ted **will have traded** his car for a new one. |

9. **The Command Form.** One more thing. Verbs also have a **command form**. The command form uses the infinitive of the verb (without *to*). It is used when asking or telling someone to do something.

Examples: | **Open** the door! |

| **Answer** the phone! |

| Please, **write** him a letter! |

The same form of the verb is used for singular or plural here. Context tells us which one we mean. When we make a strong suggestion or extend an invitation, the infinitive of the main verb is then preceded by *let's.*

Examples: | **Let's play** bingo. |

| **Let's go** to the movies. |

In summary, verbs are the second basic element in the sentence. They show action, thought, feeling and state of mind or condition. Verbs can also be recognized by the word "to" placed in front of them to indicate the infinitive, such as in "to run," and by their conjugated forms. The choice of verbs determines how our writing impacts on the reader. Knowing how to use person, number, and tense correctly makes writing not only more clear-cut, but it can add a three-dimensional quality as well. Some verbs have different functions, such as linking verbs, and knowing how to use them correctly in the sentence gives credibility to speech and writing. Helping verbs are an aid in expressing tense, but they can make writing wordy. Knowing, therefore, how to cut down on using them without losing meaning can make writing more powerful. Some verbs are irregular. Memorizing their forms, along with the linking verbs, is the only solution. Once we know how important verbs are, it's a breeze.

Exploring Language

1. Find the verbs in the poem at the beginning of the chapter.

2. Write your own verb poem. Allow yourself to be serious or funny or a bit off the wall, whatever your mood requires. But make it communicate.

3. Now write a brief essay about your favorite verb. What other verbs did you draw into the picture in the process? How would you label most of these verbs? Action? Feeling? State of being?

4. Share what you have written with a friend. Encourage him or her to voice comments. What reactions did you get?

Chapter 14
ADVERBS GIVE DIRECTION

THE AUDIENCE

When she sang softly,
the audience listened silently.

But her crescendo brought them
to their feet jubilantly.

Soon the crowd waved arms
in rhythm with the music.

Afterwards, they applauded
and cheered enthusiastically.

Adverbs add meaning to other words. The word *adverb* comes from the Latin *adverbium*, *ad* meaning *to* and *verbium* meaning *word*. They can be identified by their form, function, and meaning. An adverb can describe a verb, an adjective, another adverb, a clause, even a sentence.

Adverbs Can Be Grouped by Meaning
Adverbs answer such questions as:

How?   well, slowly, fast, carefully

How much? To what extent?   little, more, completely, totally

Where?	here, there, north, upstairs
How often?	frequently, always, never
When?	now, later, soon, afterwards
Why?	consequently, hence, accordingly, therefore
They can also assert: Yes or No	yes, perhaps, certainly, maybe

Adverbs Can Be Identified by Their Function

1. When adverbs **describe verbs**, they generally follow the verb or object in the sentence.

Examples:

John passed the ball **quickly** *John* is the subject; *the ball* is the direct object; *quickly* describes how John passed the ball.

Laura talked **occasionally**. *Laura* is the subject; *talked* is the verb; *occasionally* tells when Laura talked.

2. When adverbs **describe adjectives**, they generally precede them in the sentence. They often answer the question: To what degree?

Examples:

Her mother is a **very** pretty woman. How pretty?

The bus was **quite** late. How late?

An **unusually** cold winter is coming to an end. How cold?

3. Adverbs can describe **other adverbs**.

Examples:

He knew her **too well**.

The adverb, *too,* describes the adverb, *well.*

We visited **quite often**.
The adverb, *quite,* describes the adverb, *often.*

The fans are **already here**.
The adverb, *already,* describes the adverb, *here.*

4. Adverbs can **describe clauses or sentences**. They are then frequently off-set by a comma.

Examples:
Finally, we have spring.
The adverb, *finally,* describes the sentence, *we have spring.*

Possibly, we will see you.
The adverb, *possibly,* describes the sentence, *we will see you.*

Perhaps we should go.
The adverb, *perhaps,* describes the sentence, *we should go.*

Adverbs Can Be Identified by Their Form

1. Adverbs are often **derived from adjectives** and sometimes **from participles**. Many of these adjectives or participles simply add the ending **–ly** to become adverbs.

Examples:

Adjective	Adverb
bad	badly
beautiful	beautifully
correct	correctly
frequent	frequently
general	generally
great	greatly
intermittent	intermittently
quick	quickly
ready	readily
shocking	shockingly
strong	strongly

Participle	Adverb
admitted	admittedly
mistaken	mistakenly
supposed	supposedly

2. Some adverbs, however, add **no ending**. Some common ones are:

always	perhaps	sometimes	when
maybe	quite	somewhat	where
never	rather	then	yes
not	seldom	there	
now	since	too	

3. A number of adverbs have the **same form as adjectives.** Here are some

better	fair	much	so
bright	fast	near	straight
cheap	first	no	very
close	hard	right	well
deep	high	second	wrong
early	late	slow	
even	loud	smooth	

4. Some adverbs that are derived from adjectives have **two forms**, one **without** and the other **with the –ly ending.**

bad	doubtless	high	near
bright	even	just	right
cheap	fair	late	second
close	fast	loud	sharp
deep	first	low	wrong

Note on usage: Depending on the meaning, the short form of these adverbs may be used more likely in spoken English. The –*ly* ending form, on the other hand, may be generally preferred in written English.

Examples: He drove **slow**.

                        She talked **loud**.

Adverbs Can Be Compared

The comparison of adverbs is similar to the comparison of adjectives.

1. In the comparative, the adverb adds **–er** and in the superlative, it adds **–est.**

Positive	Comparative	Superlative
cheap	cheaper	cheapest
fast	faster	fastest
great	greater	greatest

2. When adverbs have more than one syllable, they usually use **more** and **most** to form comparative and superlative degrees.

Positive	Comparative	Superlative
slowly	more slowly	most slowly
quickly	more quickly	most quickly
easily	more easily	most easily

Sometimes Other Elements in the Sentence Can take Over an Adverbial Function

1. **Nouns** can function as adverbs. For example:

   We read **evenings**.

   Evenings is a noun telling us *when* we read.

   The children will stay **next summer**.

   Next summer is a noun phrase telling us *when* the children will stay.

2. **Phrases or clauses** can also function in an adverbial manner. For example:

   The students will depart **in a month**.

   The prepositional phrase *in a month* tells *when* students will depart.

   When it is time, they will come.

   When it is time is an adverbial clause telling *when* they will come.

As we have seen, adverbs describe verbs, adjectives and other adverbs. Many adverbs are derived from adjectives or participles. Adverbs can, therefore, often be recognized by their endings. However, not all adjectives have specific endings. Adverbs, similarly to adjectives, show degrees of comparison. Furthermore, sometimes nouns can serve as adverbs. Other times, phrases and clauses can serve as adverbs. Whew! Just follow the adverbs by their function!

Exploring Language

1. Find the adverbs in the poem at the beginning of the chapter.

2. Make a list of at least 5 adverbs that you use frequently in your speech. Compare the list with that of a friend. What is your conclusion?

3. Write a paragraph about your pet or an animal that you like. *After you are done*, underline all the adverbs in your description. What do they express about the pet's or animal's activities?

Chapter 15
PREPOSITIONS CONNECT

STAND-OFF

We talk it over
between us,
face to face.

The misunderstanding
brought us to an impasse
for the second time.

The challenge before us
is not who is right,
or who is wrong
but to see each other's
point of view
and then start
from the beginning.

Prepositions connect nouns and pronouns with other words. Actually, the word *preposition* comes from the Latin *praeponere*, to put in front. Prepositions connect words in the sentence. Understanding prepositions and prepositional phrases helps us recognize more easily the remaining words and their function in the sentence.

Prepositions May Indicate, Among Other Things, Place, Position, Destination, Direction, Source, or Means

If this sounds like a mouth full, the following explanations and examples will make it easier. To begin with, below is a list of commonly used prepositions.

about	below	inside	throughout
above	beneath	into	to
across	beside	like	toward
after	between	near	under
against	beyond	of	underneath
along	by	off	unlike
among	down	on	until
around	during	out	up
as	except	outside	upon
at	for	over	with
before	from	past	within
behind	in	through	without

Prepositions Connect Words and Help Show Relationships

A preposition may relate a noun, a phrase or clause to another part of the sentence, such as to a verb, a noun or an adjective.

Examples:

1. His friends are waiting **behind** the building.

Behind is the preposition connecting the verb *waiting* with the noun *building*.

2. The roof **of** the building collapsed.

The preposition *of* connects *roof* with *building*.

3. The candidate is strong **on** promises but short **of** resolve.

The preposition *on* connects the adjective *strong* and the noun *promises*, and the preposition *of* connects the adjective *short* and the noun *resolve*.

4. Andrew brought a note **from** her.

From is the preposition connecting the noun *note* with object pronoun *her*.

The Prepositional Phrase

A preposition that is followed by a noun or pronoun is called a prepositional phrase. The noun or pronoun, as the case may be, is then called object of the preposition. Prepositional phrases are usually modifiers.

Examples:

1. Most students went **on** the trip.

On is the preposition and *trip* is a noun and the object of the preposition; *on the trip* tells where the students went.

2. They followed the guide **up** the steps **to** the castle.

Up the steps is a prepositional phrase; *to the castle* is another prepositional phrase. The noun *steps* is object of the preposition up. The noun *castle* is object of the preposition *to*. Both phrases modify followed.

3. The guide **in** the black hat showed them the sights.

In the black hat is the prepositional phrase, and the noun *hat* is object of the preposition *in*; *in the black hat* modifies the noun *guide*.

Sometimes a Prepositional Phrase Contains Two Objects

When that happens it is called compound objects of the preposition. These may be joined by *and* or *or*.

Examples:

1. We can go either **by** boat or plane.

Boat or plane are compound objects of the preposition *by*.

2. The car **with** bucket seats and blue interior is parked here.

With bucket seats and blue interior is the prepositional phrase. *With* is the preposition. *Bucket seats and blue interior* are compound objects.

In summary, prepositions connect words and so help show relationships. They can indicate place, position, destination, direction as well as source or means. Prepositional phrases are easy to identify once we recognize the prepositions. They often help complete the thought of the sentence or phrase. Let's connect, then!

Exploring Language

1. Find the prepositions and prepositional phrases in the poem at the beginning of this chapter.

2. Study the list of prepositions in Part A of this chapter. Choose approximately five prepositions from this list. Write a short paragraph or poem on a topic of your choice, using the five prepositions you have selected. If the prepositions steer your thoughts, that's okay. Let them. See where they will take you. Be adventurous.

Chapter 16
CONJUNCTIONS JOIN

THE TEAM

Join the team
and find the action.
On the sidelines
lingers no advance.
Life's the game
that waits for no one,
not for you nor for me.

If you join
the game in progress,
you will take
your turn at bat.

When the ball flies,
cease the moment:
run for fun -
and run for life.

The word *conjunction* comes from the word *conjunct* which is derived from the Latin *coniūnctus,* meaning to join together. Conjunctions join or introduce words, groups of words, clauses, sentences. We have, basically, two distinct groups of conjunctions: coordinating and subordinating.

Coordinating Conjunctions

Coordinating conjunctions join words, groups of words and sentences that are of equal value. The most common coordinating conjunctions are:

and	or	nor	for	but	yet

Consider the following **examples**:

1. Laura **and** Scott came to the party late.
2. The guests could choose to eat inside **or** outside.
3. We brought pop, ice, **and** glasses.
4. It was quite windy, **but** some people decided to play volleyball.
5. After a while, they all went inside, **for** it started to rain.
6. The party lasted until midnight, **and** Scott and Laura were the life of the party.

In a list of three or more items, the coordinating conjunctions is preceded by a comma, as in number two above. When two sentences, each with a different subject, are joined by a coordinating conjunction, the conjunction is also preceded by a comma, as in numbers four through six above.

Subordinating Conjunctions

Subordinating conjunctions introduce and join clauses, phrases, and words. Some of the most commonly used coordinating conjunctions are:

after	as though	since	unless
although	because	so that	until
as	before	such as	when
as if	if	than	whenever
as long as	in order that	that	where
as soon as	provided that	though	wherever
			while

Consider these sentences:

> 1. **Although** we leave in three weeks, we have much work left to do.
> 2. She lost track of time, **since** she began writing the paper.
> 3. Fortunately, she sent for her passport early, **because** it can take two or more months to process.
> 4. **If** she is to be ready on time, she must prepare and plan carefully.
> 5. **As long as** Anna knows what gifts to buy, shopping should be easy.
> 6. **Unless** she makes a list, she may forget something.
> 7. George will be glad, **when** the day is finally here.

Whenever a subordinating conjunction introduces a clause, we place a comma where the two clauses meet. This happens in examples one, four, and six above. When a subordinating conjunction introduces a clause that is followed by a verb phrase to complete the sentence, the comma is placed at the end of the clause, just before the independent clause. See example number five above. When the coordinating conjunction joins the second clause to the first, the comma precedes the conjunction, making clear the division. See examples two, three, and seven above.

In summary, conjunctions are easy to spot and easy to use, once we remember a few simple rules. Coordinating conjunctions usually join words, phrases, clauses, and sentences. When they join two sentences, each with a different subject, a comma is placed before the conjunction. Subordinating conjunctions can introduce as well as join words, phrases, and clauses. Since subordinating conjunctions are introducing a dependent clause, the clause is dependent on the independent clause that follows to complete the meaning of the sentence. Conjunctions help us express ourselves in a more interesting manner by making our writing more concise and complex. They can help add variety to our sentences and free us from the repetitiveness of consecutive simple sentences. So, feel free to use conjunctions and let your writing travel to its destination!

Exploring Language

1. Find the conjunctions in the poem at the head of the chapter.

2. Look at the pairs of conjunctions below. Explain how they are different and how they are similar. Give sentence examples for your conclusions.
   if – when
   since – because
   in order that – provided that
   when – whenever
   though – although

3. Make an experiment. Write a paragraph about a travel experience or an activity you do well. After you are done, see how many conjunctions you included. If you have few or no conjunctions in your paragraph, see if you can add some, both coordinating and subordinating ones. Be sure to save your first draft, so you can compare it to your second draft. How have the conjunctions changed your paragraph? Which version do you prefer? Which is more effective? Explain your conclusions.

B. LANGUAGE STRUCTURES THAT CARRY WRITING: SENTENCE TYPES

Simple> At last, he sat behind the wheel alone.

Compound> He could see traffic lighten on the other side of the bridge, but here was his exit.

Complex> After he got that first car in his mid-teens, he changed models with the seasons of his growth, as if it were a rite of passage.

Compound-Complex> When history takes us from trackless beginnings, open country and free movement and from wagon ruts to paved roads, we wonder, awestruck, about such steady and intense advancement, and we feel winds of past and present brush over land and us, breath of life's continuity.

Introduction: Constructing Sentences

It is helpful to be aware that we use different types of language versions for different types of purposes. For example, in everyday situations at home and with our friends or coworkers, our spoken language is usually conversational. It differs to varying degrees from the written language we use. The structures we use conversationally tend to be more spontaneous and, hence more informal, and may include colloquialisms, slang, and grammatical inconsistencies. We often use words and sentence structures that express our thoughts quickly, almost automatically, without deliberation, particularly if these structures are a part of the popular language. And we accompany the spoken language with voice inflections, intonation, and gestures to accentuate our meaning.

In writing, however, it is necessary to use language structures that express clearly and accurately what we want to communicate whether we are writing a letter or business report, a memoir or novel, a book on gardening or scientific findings, a magazine article or an instruction manual. Appropriate punctuation replaces then, to some degree, voice inflections, intonation, and gestures within the sentence and between sentences to establish clarity of meaning. Since written language needs to be considerably more deliberate and organized than spoken language, it is helpful to distinguish grammatical structures. And even though written language tends to be a great deal more informal today than in the past, and even more so when used in e-mails and on social media it, nevertheless, requires accuracy, consistency, and logical, coherent development. When we understand the fundamentals of effective sentences, we are ready to embark on the actual process of writing that lets our thoughts come alive, from creative to expository to informational writing.

Good writing, to a large degree, depends on sentences that communicate information correctly and in a variety of constructions. The parts of speech we have just studied give us the language to discuss word order and the function of words as they form sentences. We are then prepared to look at what constitutes a basic sentence and progress to examining different sentence types. In the process, we also learn to punctuate by setting apart certain sentence components.

A **sentence** can be defined as **a group of words that form a grammatical unit.** A sentence generally **contains a subject and a predicate and expresses a complete thought**. The **Subject** is initiator of the action and can be a noun, pronoun, or noun phrase. The **predicate** receives the action of the subject which consists of the **direct object** and **indirect object** that follow the verb. The **direct object** receives the action of the verb (transitive) directly, and an **indirect object** follows the action of a verb indirectly. For example: The woman hands him the measuring tape. The **indirect object** also follows verbs (intransitive) that cannot take a direct object. For example: He went to the store. As we can see, sometimes indirect objects can be expressed by means of a prepositional phrase. An **object** can be a noun, pronoun, or phrase.

We can, basically, distinguish **four sentence types: simple, compound, complex, and compound-complex.** To help us further understand the make-up of sentences, we will also look at such sentence parts as **phrases and clauses** and their functions. All of this will become clear as we go.

With that in mind, let the journey begin!

Chapter 17
SIMPLE SENTENCE

The Beginning

At last, he sat behind the wheel alone. With delight, he shifted the car into gear. He accelerated from a sense of power to the energy of movement, the speed of freedom, freedom to go anywhere, anytime. The open road belonged to him now – and the sky. Everything else dropped away.

The simple sentence, as the name suggests, is the most basic of sentences. It contains one independent statement. This basic structure allows us to expand into all other sentence types. Understanding the simple sentence is, therefore, fundamental to understanding sentence construction in general. The word simple means containing one main idea only.

The simple sentence is made up of two basic elements: **a subject and a predicate**. The **subject** can be **a noun or pronoun**. It initiates the action of the sentence. The **predicate** usually contains **the verb and its modifiers, or complements, and its objects** that say something about the subject. In its most reduced form, a simple sentence can consist of just a subject and a verb. However, it can add modifiers and phrases in order to enhance meaning or complement ideas about the subject. Here are some **examples**.

Simple Sentences

1. **The boy ate**. *Boy* is the subject. *Ate* is the verb.

2. **He ate a sandwich**. *He* is the subject, *ate a sandwich* is the predicate, *ate* being the verb, *a sandwich* the direct object.

3. **Jeff had pizza for lunch today**. *Jeff* is the subject; h*ad pizza for lunch today* is the predicate, *had* being the verb, *pizza* the direct object, f*or lunch* the prepositional phrase, and *today* the adverb of time telling when.

4. **John and Laura met us at the restaurant**. *John and Laura* are compound Subject; *met us at the restaurant* is the predicate, *met* being the verb, *us* direct object, *at the restaurant* the prepositional phrase.

5. **We sang and danced all night**. *We* is the subject; *sang and danced all night* is the predicate, *sang and danced* being compound verbs, *all night* being an adverbial phrase telling when, describing both verbs.

6. **They ordered dinner and talked politics**. *They* is the subject; *ordered dinner* and *talked politics* are compound predicates; *dinner* is the direct object of the verb *ordered* and *politics* is the direct object of the verb *talked*.

7. **According to the report, the president will arrive tomorrow**. *According to the report* is a prepositional phrase introducing the subject and is, therefore, offset by a comma; *the president* is the subject; *will arrive* are verbs (helping verb and main verb respectively); *tomorrow* is an adverb of time describing the verb *arrive*.

8. **The speaker, a tall, impressive figure, lectured for an hour**. *The speaker* is the subject; *a tall, impressive figure* is an appositive (usually a noun or pronoun that follows a noun and describes it further, set off by commas to form a parenthetical construction). *Lectured for an hour* is the predicate, *lectured* being the verb, *for an hour* a prepositional phrase.

9. **Drawing and sketching are his favorite activities**. *Drawing* and *sketching* are compound subject (they are gerunds, nouns derived from verbs); *are* is the verb; *activities* is the direct object.

10. **Going to the movies has become their favorite pastime**. *Going to the movies* is the subject (*going* is the gerund, *to the movies* the prepositional phrase modifying going); *has become* are verbs; *pastime* is the direct object.

Conclusion

As we have seen, the simple sentence can have a variety of versions. The most important thing to keep in mind about the **simple sentence** is that it **consists of a subject and a predicate**. It can be as basic as just a subject and a verb, as long as the thought is complete. But it can also add different kinds of phrases serving as modifiers or complements. Therefore, some simple sentences can be very short; others can be quite lengthy. Length in itself, however, is not necessarily an indicator of a simple sentence. Yet understanding this basic sentence type will help us understand other, more complex, sentence structures.

If we were to compare the sentence to the world of automobiles, the simple sentence could be a compact car. It gets us to our destination, but we may be limited as to how many passengers or how much cargo we can carry. And while simple sentences are basic, their overuse can make writing monotonous. Nevertheless, they can, at times, be very effective in all types of writing when clarity or style are a consideration.

Now that we have the key, let's see where our new vehicle will take us!

Exploring Reading

1. In the passage at the beginning of this chapter, locate subject, verb, object, and prepositional phrase in the respective sentences.

2. In your favorite magazine or newspaper, find five simple sentences. Write down the names of your sources. Consider the purpose of these sentences.

3. In a novel or other literature, find five simple sentences. Write down the source of your sentences. Consider the effect of the sentences.

4. Explain your sentences in a group, such as a writers group or reading club. State your sources and discuss why you think the author may have chosen simple sentences to convey meaning and effect in your various readings.

Exploring Writing

1. Write five simple sentences. Vary each sentence according to length and structural content. Include such structures as direct and indirect objects, prepositional phrases and other phrases, and so on. Then label each sentence part according to subject, verb, object, prepositional phrase and so on until all main sentence parts are identified.

2. Next time you write a letter, essay, story, or poem, check your sentences. Are most of them simple? Would you like to instill more variation and vitality into your writing? Then explore the next five chapters of this section.

Chapter 18
PHRASES:
SENTENCE COMPONENTS

In the Making

The quest moves him from play with matchbook cars to draw flaming cars, then to refurbish old cars and turn them into working antiques. In seasons of exploration and growth from childhood to teenage years, he keeps on disassembling and rebuilding them. Trips to junk yard become treasure hunts. Car parts cover garage floor, awaiting installation. Upholstery re-stitched becomes a new skill acquired. A test drive, another car sold form a spiral that leads to a chosen pursuit, depicts an engineer in the making.

Phrases are important components of sentences, adding structure and meaning. **Phrases are groups of two or more words without subject or predicate**. They are units of meaning within the sentence. Phrases cannot stand independently like a sentence. They, however, follow distinct patterns that become easy to recognize once we know what they are. Being able to identify different phrases helps us understand more of the structural components of the sentence and permits us to add interest, variety and meaning.

The word **phrase** comes from the Latin *phrasis* meaning style of speech. It is derived from the Greek *phrazein* meaning to explain. The English language is open to many different kinds of phrases, depending on grammatical interpretation. For instance, *has been* is one kind of verbal phrase. In this context, we will consider three major types of phrases: prepositional phrases, verbal phrases, and appositives. A general recognition of phrases will help give us a better understanding of how we compose sentences.

Prepositional Phrases

Prepositional phrases usually start with a preposition and end in a noun or pronoun. This noun or pronoun is called object of the preposition. We have discussed prepositional phrases in Part II, A, Chapter 15 "Prepositions Connect" where a list of prepositions can be found. Prepositional phrases usually function as modifiers, such as adverbs or adjectives.

> ### Prepositional Phrases Used in Sentences
> 1. They played the game **at home**. *They* is the subject, *played* the verb, *game* the direct object, and *at home* is the prepositional phrase.
>
> 2. It started **at just the right moment**. *It* is the subject, *started* the verb, and *at just the right moment* is the prepositional phrase.
>
> 3. The fans broke **into a wild cheer**. *Fans* is the subject, *broke* the verb, and *into a wild cheer* is the prepositional phrase.
>
> 4. The opposing team scored **in a surprise move**. *Team* is the subject, *scored* the verb, and *in a surprise move* is the prepositional phrase.

Since prepositional phrases are quite common in English, it is helpful to be able to identify them in the sentence, particularly when we try to establish the various sentence components. Once they are identified, we can more easily distinguish other major sentence components and parts.

Verbal Phrases

There are a number of verbal phrases. For instance, we can consider **am going** or **have been eating** verbal phrases. These particular verbal phrases express tense of verb and continuity of action. But these are not our concern here. In this section, we will discuss verbal phrases that serve either to complete or modify another word or structure in the sentence. Often, those types of verbs do not act as verbs but as another part of speech, such as a noun, an adjective, or adverb. The derived words are then called **verbals**. We will consider three **verbal phrases** here: **infinitive, gerund, and participial**.

Infinitive Phrases. These involve the infinitive of a verb. As we have seen earlier, the infinitive form of a verb is the base form of the verb preceded by **to** (although that is not usually shown)**: to sleep, to walk, to dream**, for example. **Followed by modifiers, the infinitive becomes an infinitive phrase**. In this context, the infinitive can serve as noun, adjective or adverb.

Infinitive Phrases Used in Sentences
a. **To visit periodically** is her goal. The phrase serves as subject.

b. She promised **to come this summer**. The phrase serves as indirect object.

c. Her intent is **to learn German well**. The phrase serves as predicate noun.

d. The opportunity **to speak often** is the advantage of staying longer. The phrase serves as adjective describing the noun *opportunity*.

e. A low fare is helpful **to keep expenses down**. The phrase serves as adverb describing the adjective *helpful*.

Another thing to remember is that it is preferable not to split the infinitive in the sentence.

For example:

Awkward	Correct
to easily manage	to manage easily
to narrowly miss	to miss narrowly
to better understand	to understand better

Gerund Phrases. As we have seen earlier, gerunds are verbs ending in *–ing* (present participles) used as nouns. For example:

Scoring became more important than play.
Scoring is the gerund serving as subject in this sentence.

When **a gerund is accompanied by modifiers, it is a gerund phrase**. A gerund phrase (or gerund) can serve different functions in the sentence. It can serve as subject, predicate noun, direct or indirect object, even as object of a preposition. For example:

Gerund Phrases Used in Sentences

a. **Refurbishing cars** is his favorite occupation. The gerund phrase serves as subject.

b. He began **the rebuilding process** at fourteen. Here it serves as direct object.

c. The young man spends many hours **working in the garage**. Gerund phrase indirect object.

d. **By working regularly**, he has restored many antiques. Gerund phrase as object of the preposition *by*.

e. His greatest reward is **showing in antique car shows**. Gerund phrase as predicate noun.

Participial Phrases. Participles of verbs often serve as adjectives. We have seen in Part II, A, Chapter 13 "Verbs Move Body and Mind," that present participles end in *–ing*, such as *walking*. Past participles can end in *-ed*, such as walked, *-t* in sent, *-en* in gotten, and occasionally in *–d* as in heard, or *–n* as in won.

For example:

a. The **waiting** crowd milled around. *Waiting* is the present participle of 'wait,'

b. used as adjective. The **hidden** sun sent beams between clouds. *Hidden* is the past participle of 'hide,' used as adjective. Participles initiate a **participial phrase when they add other words that serve as modifiers**.

Participial Phrases Used in Sentences

a. The crowd, **waiting patiently**, milled around. *Waiting patiently* is the participial phrase describing *crowd*.

b. The performance, **delayed for an hour**, finally began. *Delayed for an hour* is the participial phrase describing *performance*.

c. **Walking swiftly onto the stage**, the performers greeted the audience. *Walking swiftly onto the stage* is a participial phrase describing *performers*.

Note that participial phrases are frequently offset by commas. Participial phrases can also contain prepositional phrases, as in c above, where *onto the stage* is the prepositional phrase. Finally, participial phrases must be close to the word or words they modify to avoid confusion. For example:

Wrong   The audience watched intensely as performers played their instruments, **clapping to the beat**. *Clapping to the beat* is the participial phrase. Its location would have it describe instruments. But since instruments cannot clap, the phrase is misplaced. The modifier, namely the participial phrase, needs to be close to the word *audience*. The sentence should read:

Correct   **Clapping to the** beat, the audience watched intensely as performers played their instruments.

Appositive Phrases

An appositive is a word or phrase that is in apposition. The word apposition comes from the Latin and means to place near. An appositive is a noun or pronoun that describes another word next to it. For example:

His friend, **Eric**, lives down the block.

An **appositive phrase** is one in which **a noun or pronoun and their modifiers describe another noun or pronoun**. The appositive phrase also generally follows the noun or pronoun. It is usually offset by a comma or commas. When the appositive phrase is removed, it does not generally affect the structure or meaning of the sentence.

Examples:
1. Laura, **first in line**, bought the tickets.

2. The movie, **a gothic thriller**, lasted two hours.

3. The audience, **mostly high school students**, reacted loudly.

4. They all stopped at the fast food restaurant, **their favorite gathering place**.

Conclusion

Phrases are two or more words that do not have a subject or a predicate. In this chapter, we have distinguished three major types of phrases, namely: prepositional, verbal, and appositive. Probably the most frequently occurring type of phrase is the prepositional phrase. It is, therefore, particularly helpful to be well acquainted with it. Having at least an awareness of verbal phrases and how they function is useful in knowing what else is going on in the sentence. Appositive phrases are easy to spot because of their parenthetical nature.

So now that we have more components, let's assemble the whole!

Exploring Writing

1. Can you find the phrases in the passage at the top of the page? Write them down in your notebook and discuss them with a cohort.

2. Write a number of sentences for each type of phrase discussed in this chapter:
   a. The prepositional phrase. Be sure to use a variety of prepositions.

   b. The appositive phrase. Vary the phrases using nouns and pronouns.

   c. Verbal phrases. Be sure to include at least one sentence for each of the following types of verbal phrases:

      (1) Infinitive phrase.
      (2) Gerund phrase.
      (3) Participial phrase.

Chapter 19
COMPOUND SENTENCE

Connection

He watched the red Mustang gain behind him; it sped along, switching lanes, overtaking. inching along on the congested freeway. He thought, driving slowly was for a minivan, a Chevy Taho, or a school bus, but it was not for the semi passing just behind him in the left lane or his Jeep, for that matter. The Mustang suddenly squeezed in front of him, with barely an inch between them. He would have liked to show it real speed, but at that moment, nothing less than a tank or helicopter would have done, here, in this solid stream of rush-hour cars ahead. Doggedly, the Mustang hugged the bumper in front of it, holding the space like a birth right not to be relinquished, not even to vehicles trying to merge from ramps. He could see traffic loosen into a third lane on the other side of the bridge, but here was his exit. He noticed the Mustang gain speed, leaving him far behind, the female driver's long blond hair streaming out the open window like a banner, combustion of eons spurring it on.

To compound means to join together two or more items of equal value. **A compound sentence joins together two or more independent clauses or sentences to form a single sentence.** The sentences joined can be either simple or complex. This joining can be accomplished in two ways:

Combining Sentences Using a Coordinating Conjunction

Coordinating refers to arranging structures of equal value. **Conjunction** refers to joining or bringing together. The most common coordinating conjunctions, as we have seen earlier, are:

and	**or**	**nor**	**for**	**but**

Less commonly used coordinating conjunctions are:

yet	**only**	**while**

Usage Note: The conjunction *while* can also be a subordinating conjunction. For example: *While she loves flowers, she has no knack for growing them.* Here it is to mean "though" and is thus used as a subordinating conjunction. When, occasionally, it is used to mean *but* or *and*, then it is used as a coordinating conjunction, for example: *The violet is wilting, while the orchid is blooming.*

When two sentence parts are joined by a coordinating conjunction, the coordinating conjunction is preceded by a comma. The following examples use a variety of simple sentences to combine them into compound sentences:

1. **He went into the store, and the clerk filled his order**. *He went into the store* marks the first sentence [actually a clause here]. The subject is *he*; the verb is *went*; *into the store* is the prepositional phrase. *The clerk filled his order* marks the second clause, *clerk* is the subject; *filled* is the verb; *his order* is the direct object. The two sentences are joined by the coordinating conjunction *and* preceded by a comma.

2. **Jane will call, or the meeting is off**. *Jane will call* marks the first clause. *Jane* is the subject; *will call* are helping verb and main verb, respectively. *The meeting is off* marks the second clause; *meeting* is the subject; *is* is the verb; *off* is a predicate adjective here; *or* is the coordinating conjunction combining the two sentence parts preceded by a comma.

3. **The children and the dog ran to the corner, but the traffic light still had not changed**. The *children and the dog ran to the corner* mark the first

clause. *The children and the dog* are the compound subject; *ran* is the verb; *to the corner* is the prepositional phrase; *the traffic light still had not changed* marks the second clause; *traffic light* is the subject; *had changed* are helping verb and main verb; *not* is the adverb describing *changed*. The two clauses are combined using the coordinating conjunction *but* preceded by a comma.

4. **She wanted to hand out prizes, *only* she forgot to put them into her bag.** Here *only* is used like *but* and combines the independent sentence parts, *she wanted to hand out prizes,* and *she forgot to put them into her bag.*

5. **The first performer was a singer, *while* the second was an acrobat.** *While,* here, actually means 'but.'. It is used to join the independent sentence parts, *The first performer was a singer* and *the second was an acrobat.*

Note: When we join two sentences without benefit of coordinating conjunction after the comma, we have a run-on sentence. For example:

Run-On Sentence
   The storm broke on Monday, by Tuesday the skies cleared.
Because there is no coordinating conjunction between the first sentence and the second, we have a **run-on sentence.**

Right
   The storm broke on Monday, *but* by Tuesday the skies cleared.
The coordinating conjunction *but* joins our two clauses, preceded by a comma.

Combining Sentences with a Semicolon
Another way to create a compound sentence is with the use of a semicolon. This can be done with or without the use of a coordinating conjunction. The two sentences have to be closely related in meaning, however. A period between them would be too much of a separation, and therefore, a semicolon would be preferred.

1. **Traffic slowed down steadily; it was approaching the bridge.** *Traffic slowed down steadily* marks the first clause. *Traffic* is the subject; *slowed down* is the verb. *It was approaching the bridge* is the second independent sentence.

It is the subject; *approaching* is the verb; *bridge* is the direct object. The *semi-colon* marks the point where the two structures are joined.

2. **He did not phone; the answer would have to wait.**
    He did not phone is the first clause. *He* is the subject; *did phone* are helping verb and verb respectively; *not* is an adverb; *the answer would have to wait* marks the second clause; *the answer* is the subject; *would have to wait* is a verb phrase. The *semicolon* is placed at the point of juncture.

Avoiding Wordiness in Compound Sentences

Still another thing to keep in mind when writing compound sentences is to **avoid wordiness**. If the subject of the compound sentence parts (or clauses) is identical, then the preferred structure may not be a compound sentence but a compound verb by omitting the repetition of the subject in the second part. This tightens the sentence by avoiding unnecessary repetition. The end result may not give us a compound sentence but a tighter sentence structure which is preferred in any case, as explained below.

Example 1:
   Compound sentence
   Wordy   **Scott opened the letter, and he read it quickly.**
                     Scott in the first half of the compound refers to the same person as *he* in the second part.

   Compound predicate
   Tightened   **Scott opened the letter and read it quickly**.
                     Scott now is the only subject in the sentence. *Opened* is the first verb with its direct object, *the letter*. This is followed by the co-ordinating conjunction, *and*. The conjunction joins the second verb, *read*, and its direct object, *it*. The comma is now omitted, because we no longer have two distinct structures but merely one. This gives us instead of a compound sentence a compound predicate.

Example 2:
   Compound sentence
   Wordy   **Laura went to the store, and she bought milk and cookies.**

Laura refers to the same person as *she* in the second clause. *Laura* and *she* are each subject of their respective clauses.

Compound verb structure:

Tightened   **Laura went to the store and bought milk and cookies.**

Laura is now the only subject in the sentence. *Went* is the first verb; *to the store* is a prepositional phrase; *and* is the coordinating conjunction, joining *bought*, the second verb and its direct objects, also compounds, *milk and cookies*. Still, the meaning is clear without the addition of *she*.

Conclusion

Compound sentences can consist of separate independent clauses (or sentences), combined with coordinating conjunctions. Sometimes semicolons can be used between clauses, especially when there is no coordinating conjunction and particularly when the ideas of the clauses are all closely related. The compound sentence is one that expands beyond the simple sentence, combining two or more ideas. This type of sentence adds interest to our writing as well as variety.

The compound sentence is like moving toward a mid-size car. It has all the features of the compact version, but there is more room to stretch. Oh, let us see how this vehicle will get us to our destination more comfortably!

Exploring Writing

1. Read the selection at the beginning of the chapter. Find the compound sentences. To help with this task, find, first, subjects and verbs in the sentences. Then, find prepositional phrases. Third, look for coordinating conjunctions and semicolons.

2. Write five compound sentences, three of these using coordinating conjunctions and two using semicolons. Label each clause according to subject, verb, object, and prepositional phrase.

3. In your reading, whether that is a news report, magazine or book, see if you can find five compound sentences. Mark and compare them. Then discuss your findings with a cohort.

4. In your writing, include some compound sentences. Check your sentences when you write. Are you using a lot of simple sentences? If so, see if you can combine some of them to form compound sentences. Remember to reduce wordiness. See if tightening does not make your writing more interesting.

Chapter 20
CLAUSES: MORE SENTENCE COMPONENTS

Seeking Connection

When the light changed, the red Mustang slowly rounded the busy corner on its way around the block. The car pulsated to the sound of percussion coming from its interior, the driver's arm dangling casually out the window. Traffic nervously steered around the Mustang, its driver oblivious, intent – absorbed in the surroundings as if looking for someone or something. Arriving at the same light again, she pulled in the arm to fix her face, leaning toward the rear-view mirror, adjusting it to see herself. On green, she began cruising once more, eyes scanning left to right, left to right, and then she rounded the corner still another time, slowly, very slowly, closing the circle.

The word *clause* comes from the Latin *claudere* meaning to close. **A clause is a group of words consisting of a subject and a predicate**. A clause can be **dependent or independent**. The following sentences are made up of two clauses, one independent and the other dependent. An **independent clause could stand alone** as a sentence. But **a dependent clause cannot stand alone**. The dependent clause is bound to the independent clause to complete its meaning. It is often introduced by means of a subordinating conjunction or relative pronoun. Consider the following **examples:**

1. **The sun was shining when we mowed the lawn.**
   Independent Clause

The sun was shining... *Sun* is the subject; *was shining* are predicate verbs. This structure could stand alone as a sentence. Its meaning is complete.

Dependent Clause

...when we mowed the lawn. This is the dependent clause introduced by the subordinating conjunction *when*. It leans on the independent clause to complete its meaning.

2. **Before it rained, the children played outside.**

   Dependent Clause

   Before it rained... The sentence begins with the dependent clause, introduced with the subordinating conjunction *before*. The subject is *it*, the verb is *rained*. The thought of the clause has yet to be completed.

   Independent Clause

   ...the children played outside. This is the independent clause. It could stand alone as a sentence. *Children* is the subject; *played outside* is the predicate.

When we take a closer look at clauses, we can distinguish three types of dependent clauses: noun clauses, adjective clauses, and adverb clauses.

Noun Clauses

A noun clause, as the name suggests, **functions as a noun** in the sentence. A noun clause may be **used as subject, object of a verb or preposition, or predicate noun**. A noun clause is usually introduced by a relative pronoun. A relative pronoun generally refers to an antecedent, a word, phrase or clause going before. Sometimes other connectives, such as when, whenever, where, or why may be used.

Relative Pronouns

who	which	that	what
whoever	whose		whatever
whom			
whomever			
whose			

A Note on the use of the relative pronouns who and whom, whoever and whomever: Traditional grammar has required that *who* and *whoever* be used as subject in the sentence and *whom* and *whomever* be used as object. However, in today's spoken language *who* and *whoever* are both used as subject and object in the sentence in order not to sound stuffy. In formal or written language, the traditional forms are more likely to be used, however. In a sense, it becomes a writer's choice.

Here are some examples of relative pronouns used in sentences:

1. **Whoever had the idea** must explain it to the group.
   The clause introduced by *whoever* is the **subject**.
2. He promised **that they would leave as soon as possible**.
   The clause introduced by *that* is the **object**.
3. John prepared them for **what lay ahead**.
   The clause introduced by *what* is **subject of the preposition** *for*.
4. The path is **where we are standing**.
   The clause introduced by *where* is the **predicate noun**.

Adjective Clauses

Adjective clauses **describe nouns or pronouns**. In this sense, they work like adjectives. Usually, adjective clauses are introduced with relative pronouns, sometimes with other connectives. At other times, when the connective word is not necessary for meaning or structure, it can be omitted.

1. It was the day **that brought great change.** The dependent clause introduced by *that* describes the noun *day*.

2. Students **who attended the lecture** felt enlightened. The dependent clause introduced by *who* describes the noun *students*.

3. Those **whose views conflicted** left early. The dependent clause introduced by *whose* describes the pronoun *those*.

4. The time **when students followed blindly** had passed. The dependent clause introduced by *when* describes the noun *time*.

5. The topic led to a long discussion **which ended at midnight**. The dependent clause introduced by *which* describes the noun *discussion*.

6. It was an event **the instructor had not anticipated**. The introductory relat-

ive pronoun *that* can be omitted from the dependent clause, because it is understood, reducing wordiness. Otherwise, the sentence would read: *It was an event **that** the instructor had not anticipated.*

Adjective clauses that do not affect the meaning of the sentence are set off by commas.

1. The guests**, who came from other states,** had participated in the lively exchange.

2. The night**, which promised to be long,** was warm and humid.

Adverb Clauses

Adverb dependent clauses **serve as adverbial modifiers**. Therefore, they tell when, where, how, why, to what extent. Adverb dependent clauses begin with subordinating conjunctions. The most frequently used ones, as we have seen in Part II, A, Chapter 16 "Conjunctions Join," are listed below. Notice that usually, when adverb dependent clauses begin the sentence, they are followed by a comma.

Subordinating Conjunctions

after	as though	since	when
although	because	so that	whenever
as	before	such as	where
as if	if	though	wherever
as long as	in order that	unless	while
as soon as	provided that	until	

Examples:
1. **When the tornado struck,** the family was alarmed.
   The dependent clause introduced by *when* **describes the adjective** *alarmed.*
2. It seemed **as if some magic power had uprooted the great oak.**
   The dependent clause introduced by *as if* **describes the verb** *seemed.*

3. **If relief arrives,** they will rebuild soon.
   The dependent clause introduced by *if* **describes the adverb** *soon.*

4. They felt hopeful, **because many people offered help.**

The dependent clause introduced by *because* **describes the adjective** *hopeful*.

Adverb dependent clauses can have elliptical constructions. An **ellipsis** refers to a construction where **a word or words have been omitted** because the meaning is clear without them, or because they may have been implied by another construction in the sentence.

1. **While waiting for the storm to pass,** they heard the sound of a thundering freight train. The dependent clause introduced by *while* describes the verb *heard*. *While waiting* is an *elliptical* construction. The clause, without omissions, might have read: *While **they were** waiting for the storm to pass.* **They** is implied by the independent clause that follows and is therefore not necessary for the meaning and neither is the helping verb *were*.

2. **When surveying the damage,** the contractor wrote an estimate. When introduces the adverb dependent clause. It is an *elliptical* structure which, in its complete form, would read: *When **the contractor was** surveying the damage.* But since the meaning is clear without these words, we omit them.

Conclusion
The most important thing to remember about a clause is that it is a group of words comprised of a subject and a predicate. Independent clauses can stand alone as sentences. Dependent clauses lean on independent clauses to convey a complete thought. For the most part, dependent clauses begin with relative pronouns or subordinating conjunctions, sometimes with other connectives. It is helpful to be able to recognize the different dependent clauses. It is also helpful to know that the introductory word or other words in the dependent clause can be omitted, at times. The more we know about clauses the better we will be at constructing sentences.

These are some of the major parts for the vehicle of our choice. Let's see how we will assemble them!

Exploring Writing

1. Can you separate the clauses in the passage at the beginning of the chapter? Looking for subordinating conjunctions and relative pronouns can be helpful in identifying clauses, since they frequently introduce them.

2. Write ten sentences that include a dependent clause each. Be sure to include a different type of clause in each of your sentences. Use each type of dependent clause we have studied, including those with elliptical constructions or word omissions. Don't forget to check on the commas.

Chapter 21
COMPLEX SENTENCE

Moving On

After he got that first car in his mid-teens, he changed models with the season of his growth, as if it were a rite of passage. The cars were reminiscent of the small models he made as a young boy and lined up on his bookshelf. Only now they line up big in the driveway. From Olds to Challenger to Charger, which he owned consecutively and on which he worked in high school, he moved to minivan and pick-up in college, until nothing but a diesel truck would do, brand new, too, with leather upholstery, because, at last, his income as a beginning engineer would allow it. When he elevated it up with big tires for easier maneuvering across country, he rode well above the rest of the world, roar of diesel engine commanding the road.

The American Heritage Dictionary defines *complex* as "consisting of interconnected or interwoven parts," a whole "composed of two or more units." The word is derived from the Latin *complexus* meaning to entwine. **A complex sentence contains one independent clause and one or more dependent clauses. An independent clause can usually stand alone as a sentence. A dependent clause is usually related to the independent clause by a relative pronoun or subordinating conjunction.** (Actually, there are many possibilities.) As we have seen in the previous chapter "Clauses: More Sentence Components," there are primarily three types of dependent clauses: noun clauses, adjective clauses, and adverb clauses. Reviewing these, the relative pronouns (see Part II, A, Chapter 20, "Clauses, More Sentence Components") and subordinating conjunctions (see Part II, A Chapter 16, "Conjunctions

Join") will help with the construction of complex sentences. The previous chapter on clauses gives us all the parts to construct a complex sentence. You may want to refer to it, particularly for the relative pronouns and subordinating conjunctions, to help you along the way. Remember the basic concept: **a clause consists of a subject and a predicate.**

Adjective Dependent Clauses

Adjective dependent clauses describe a noun. Most frequently, adjective dependent clauses begin with relative pronouns. At other times, they can begin with *when* or *where.* An adjective dependent clause that is not necessary to the meaning of the sentence is set off by a comma.

             S   V   S   V

1. **He was the boy [who wrote the paper].**
   Independent Clause   Dependent Clause

            S   S   V   V

2. **The student [whom they asked many questions] was finished.**
   The student was finished is the Independent Clause.
   ...whom they asked many questions is the Dependent Clause.

          S   V   V

3. **[Whoever wants to go to college] must take the necessary courses.**
   Dependent Clause (serves as subject)   Independent Clause

    S   V   S   V

4. **We discovered today [(that) the math requirement has been raised].**
   Independent Clause   Dependent Clause

 S V   S   V

5. **It was a time [when the country wanted change].**
   Independent Clause   Dependent Clause

Adverb Dependent Clauses

These begin with subordinating conjunctions. The subordinating conjunctions make the clause dependent. When adverb dependent clauses begin a sentence, they are followed by a comma.

$$\text{V} \qquad \text{S} \qquad \text{V}$$

1. **[While studying,] they discovered new things.**
   Dependent Clause · · · · · · · · · · Independent Clause

$$\text{S} \qquad \text{V} \qquad\qquad\qquad \text{S} \qquad \text{V}$$

2. **[After he published his first book,] he invited his friends for a celebration.**
   Dependent Clause · · · · · · · · · · · · · · · · · · Independent Clause

$$\text{S} \qquad \text{V} \qquad\quad \text{S} \qquad \text{V}$$

3. **[If my recollection is correct,] they worked on the paper all day.**
   Dependent Clause · · · · · · · · · · Independent Clause

$$\text{S} \qquad \text{V} \quad \text{S} \qquad \text{V}$$

4. **[As soon as the snow melts,] we will resume our walks in the park.**
   Dependent Clause · · · · · · · · · · Independent Clause

Noun Dependent Clauses

These serve the sentence the same way nouns or gerunds can. Therefore, noun clauses can be subject, direct object, indirect object, predicate noun, or object of the preposition.

1. **Whoever is nominated] will serve as president.**
   Noun Clause: Subject

2. **The many lakes are [what draws visitors to Minnesota.]**
   Noun clause: Predicate Noun

3. **They had no idea [that stores closed early.]**
   Noun Clause: Direct object

4. **She will distribute handouts [whenever it is necessary.]**
   Noun Clause: Indirect object

5. They award prizes [to whomever they choose].

Noun Clause: Object of the preposition

Conclusion

The complex sentence is generally made up of two clauses, an independent clause and a dependent clause. The clauses are often joined by a connective word, such as a relative pronoun or a subordinating conjunction. Each of the clauses usually has a subject and a predicate. When an adverb dependent clause begins the sentence, it is followed by a comma. When an adjective dependent clause is not necessary to the meaning of a sentence, it is set off by commas.

We are moving up in the world. Let us think of a complex sentence as a full-size car. It is roomier and more luxurious than our earlier models. Ah, what a way to travel now that we know how the parts work.

Exploring Writing

1. Find the complex sentences in the beginning passage of this chapter. Look for subordinating conjunctions and other words, such as relative pronouns, that often head clauses. Also, find the subject and verb of each clause. Put brackets around the clauses and underline the subordinating conjunctions.

2. Write ten complex sentences:

    a. Make up at least three sentences with each of the three types of clauses.

    b. Put brackets around each dependent clause.

    c. Mark the subject and verb of each clause.

3. See if you can identify complex sentences in your reading.

    a. Turn to your favorite reading and find five complex sentences and mark them.

    b. Share your sentences in a group and explain why they are complex and what makes them appropriate, desirable, or difficult in the passages from which they are taken.

4. Note the effect complex sentences have on your own writing. If you have not already made them a regular part of your writing, work on doing so whenever desirable. See how they affect the outcome of reports, papers, letters, and creative writing. When do they work best?

Chapter 22
COMPOUND-COMPLEX SENTENCE

The Trek

Under dome of Wyoming sky, rolling plains unfold the story of wagon ruts that span thousands of miles, a fading blueprint of people moving West. Our view reveals ruts interrupted by rocks, between which a tree found room to grow; ruts pick up again where rocks end on the other side of the hill, as we imagine how these travelers moved their wagons across this rugged terrain. We listen to the sound of the wind, as if for voices of the past directing wagons, hoisting, easing, whistles spurring on teams of horses.

We listen to the wind's song which seems to have carried us here, wind that seems to whisper of the past but, instead, reveals muffled voices of our children exploring tracks on their own, and we linger as if we waited long enough, we would hear peoples of past centuries in their daily activities, bison and horses pounding earth. From trackless beginnings to trails to treks to paved roads, remnants of the old Oregon Trail still stretch silently across country, leaving us to ponder history's journey to the present. The sound of a plane draws us into jet stream thoughts into the future, while we stand near our car in a moment's eternity, emblem of our own silent, invisible journey, and wind brushes over land and us, breath of life's continuity.

The Compound-Complex Sentence

The last sentence type we will consider is the compound-complex sentence. It is not used very often, because English generally likes to stay away from long sentences. Still, there are times when they are useful and stylistically desirable. **The compound-complex sentence is made up of two or more independent clauses and one or more dependent clauses.** Consequently, as we have seen before, this type of construction can include relative pronouns, subordinating as well as coordinating conjunctions to join clauses. A comma is placed between the two main sentence parts, as the examples will show. Let's consider these examples:

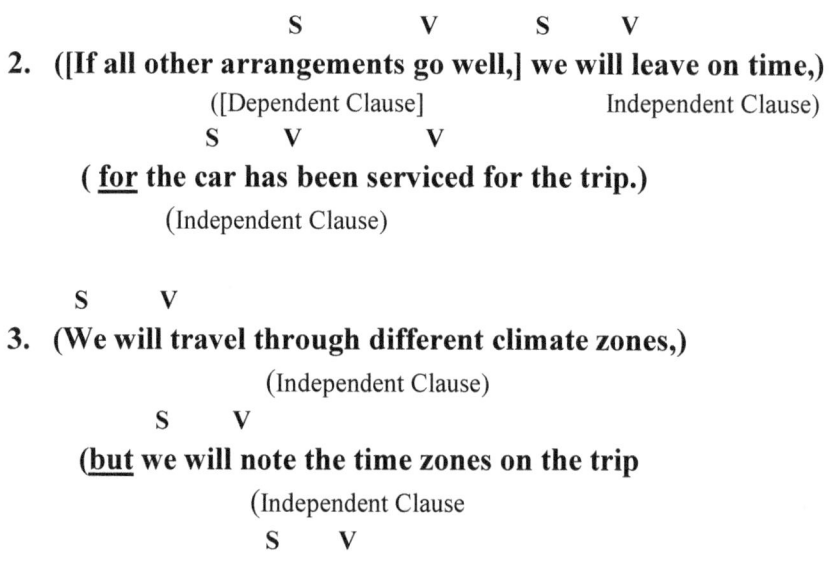

1. **(The overland trip will take a week,) (and the map [that the**
    (Independent Clause)   (Independent Clause [Dependent
    tourist office sent] shows the route.)
    Clause]   (Indep. Clause completed)

The overland trip will take a week is the first independent clause. It is
followed by a comma and the coordinating conjunction *and; and the map
shows the route* is the second independent clause; t*hat the tourist office
sent* is its dependent clause, introduced by the relative pronoun *that.*

2. **([If all other arrangements go well,] we will leave on time,)**
    ([Dependent Clause]   Independent Clause)
    (for the car has been serviced for the trip.)
    (Independent Clause)

3. **(We will travel through different climate zones,)**
    (Independent Clause)
    (but we will note the time zones on the trip
    (Independent Clause
    S   V

[in order that we arrive on time in each location.])

[Dependent Clause])

      S   V   S   V

4. **(We can stop [if we notice interesting sights,])**

    (Independent Clause   [Dependent Clause]

       S   V

(<u>but</u> we will stay on the main route.)

    (Independent Clause)

Conclusion

As we have seen, the compound-complex sentence can include all the features of phrases, clauses and sentences that we have discussed. It can be made up of two or more main clauses and one or more dependent clauses. The compound-complex sentence is the longest, most involved of all constructions we have studied. Even though it is relatively easy to write, it should be used with care and not too frequently because of its length.

Because the compound-complex sentence can include so much, we can compare it to a van or truck. Now that we are prepared for every need and occasion, let us travel the road of successful writing!

Exploring Writing

1. In the passage at the beginning of the chapter, find the compound-complex sentences as well as any of the other sentence types and mark them. Then label them according to the directions below:
    a. Put parentheses around the main clauses of the sentence.
    b. Mark the dependent clauses by putting brackets around them.
    c. Underline coordinating conjunctions and double underline subordinating conjunctions.
    d. Label the subjects and verbs of all clauses.
    e. Finally, label each dependent and each independent clause.

2. Write five compound-complex sentences.
    a. Be sure to use a different coordinating conjunction for each sentence.
    b. Also, use a variety of relative pronouns and subordinating conjunctions whenever possible.
    c. Now label your sentences according to the directions in number one above.

3. In your reading, find the compound-complex sentences and mark them. How frequently do you find them present?

4. Explain the sentences in your study group and compare what you have.

Chapter 23
PUNCTUATION REVISITED

Voice inflections, volume, gestures, and other body language clarify our speech. Standard punctuation takes the place of these to clarify writing. In this section, punctuation marks are listed with definitions and examples. However, for the placement of periods, commas, and semicolons, see the chapters on sentence types above, as these may add clarity with their particular details and examples.

Apostrophes (')
An apostrophe has these functions:

1. It is used as a contraction, meaning a letter or letters have been omitted. For example:
   a. *don't* is a contraction of **do not.**
   b. *won't* is a contraction of **will not**
2. An apostrophe is used to indicate possession. For example, *Mike's voice, Jenny's bike. the birds' refuge.* (Note: When we refer to dates, such as *in the 1990s,* no apostrophe is required, because the *s* denotes plural here, not possession.)
3. It is sometimes used to set off a quote within a quote.

Brackets [ ]
Brackets have a similar function as parentheses, but they are used when something or an explanation is added to quoted material. For example: "A wolf attacked campers in Banff National Park [near Lake Louise, in Canada] on August 9," Jenny read from the *Pioneer Press.*

Colons (:)

The colon is used in the following ways:
1. To introduce a topic or listing.
2. To introduce a quotation.
3. In a bibliography after stating the city, then the publisher. For example, New York: PALGRAVE MACMILLAN.
4. After a greeting on a formal business letter. For example, *Dear Sir/Madam:* or *Dear Ms. Jones:*
5. Between the hour and minutes when stating time. For example, 10:30.

Commas (,)

The comma is chiefly used for clarity within the sentence. For more specific information, please refer to the chapters on sentence types above. Here are some main functions:
1. To separate parts of a sentence, such as clauses, phrases, and parenthetical constructions. (Note: a comma cannot be used to end a sentence.)
2. To separate entries in a listing.
3. After an informal greeting. For example, *Hi Laura, Dear Mom,*

Dashes (–)

Dashes are not frequently used, but when they are, they indicate a break or space in time.
1. *The artist was absorbed in the scene – the way she remembered him being absorbed – his memory drawing momentum for her work.*
2. A dash can be used at the end of a sentence for a thought pause.

Hyphens (-)

Hyphens are used to combine words, sometimes of different parts of speech, to create new words. On occasion, words may add a prefix to form a new word.
1. Noun: African-American
2. Adjective: brick-and-mortar
3. Adjective: red-blooded
4. Transitive verb: deep-fry
5. Transitive verb: re-examine

Italics (*Italics*)

Italics are generally used for titles of books, plays, movies, documentaries and names of magazines, journals, and newspapers. (All of these are underlined when italics are not available.)

Parentheses ( )

Parentheses can be used as an aside to the main text as follows:

1. In brief asides of clarification, minor additional or relevant detail.
   For example: We found the discussion of the book (recommended by Kim) *Anne Morrow Lindbergh: First Lady of the Air,* most elucidating.
2. To set off numerals.
   For example: 1), 2), 3).
3. In parenthetical documentation:
   a. Inside a text after the reference: (Winters 30).
   b. Or at the end of a passage that is set off, when the parenthetical reference, such as author or title of book and page number follows the period.

Periods (.)

A period is an end stop and is used in a number of ways:

1. The period is used at the end of a complete sentence as a full stop. (See chapters on sentence types above for a further description and/or examples.)
2. It is used for listings, such as after a number or letter in such a listing.
3. It can be used in a list, after an entry to denote completion.
4. In MLA documentation between items and at the end of a bibliography listing.

Quotation Marks (")

Quotation marks are used when quoting word for word what someone said or wrote. Here is how they are used:

1. The quote may be introduced and followed by commas within the statement.
   For example:
   a. *The scientist said, "We are experiencing global warming at this time."*
   b. *"This is a serious problem," she said, "one which is affecting our future."*
      Note: *"she said"* becomes part of the sentence and is, therefore, not

capitalized. And because the quote continues after *she said,* beginning marks are placed in front of *"one…"* and closes at the end of the sentence.

   c. The teacher said, *"she turned out to be an extraordinary student."*

2. Mention of a story within a newspaper or magazine or a poem will generally be placed in quotation marks. For example: On August 16, the *Pioneer Press* published a story entitled "Como Zoo celebrates a bouncing baby puffin."

3. Closing quotation marks always follow end punctuation, whether comma, period, question mark, or exclamation point.
(Note: When paraphrasing what someone said or wrote, quotation marks are not used even though credit needs to be given at the end of the passage.)

Semicolons (;)

A semicolon functions similarly to a period, but it is weaker. Yet it is stronger than a comma. Here are some uses of the semicolon:

1. A semicolon, most frequently, joins two independent clauses or sentences that are closely related in meaning. For example: *Today the city council outlined the new tax proposal for approval; the vote that followed was unanimous.*

2. The semicolon can also be used in a sentence that carries listings of phrases for the sake of clarity, particularly if there already are commas in the sentence, such as in the following example: *The meeting was attended by the president of the organization, head trouble shooter, a Ph. D. and outspoken critic of the new approach; a member at large; the vice president and program chair; the secretary, a staunch opponent of the new plan; a journalist of the Science Monitor; and an invited audience of concerned citizens.*

Note: Creative writing may choose to deviate from the standards of good language and adequate punctuation, especially if a particular effect or style is desirable or when citing quotations for the sake of authenticity. Thus, deviations become, on occasions, exceptions of style and effect.

Appendix
IRREGULAR VERBS CHART

As we will see in the chart below, these irregular verbs do not usually add *-ed* to the stem of the verb to form the past tense. Instead, their past tense is often formed by changing the vowel of the verb root. Sometimes, the change in the past tense is so extreme, as we have seen, that it appears like a different word altogether. While the present participle of irregular verbs is also formed the by adding *-ing* to the root of the verb, the past participle, on the other hand, may carry a vowel change and end in *-d, -e, -g, -en, -n*, or *–t* most frequently, for example. While some of the verbs are part of a pattern, changes are often unpredictable. That is why it is helpful to have a verb chart available for reference or, better yet, for memorization of the principal parts of irregular verbs.

The chart below lists many of the verbs that deviate from the normal form for various reasons. The verbs have been alphabetized and then roughly grouped by similarity of patterns in their endings for greater ease of retention. Forms in parentheses are less common, particularly in writing.

Principal Parts of Some Irregular Verbs

Infinitive	Past Tense	Past Participle
dive	dived (dove)	dived (dove)
dream	dreamed (dreamt)	dreamed (dreamt)
feed	fed	fed
flee	fled	fled
have	had	had
hear	heard	heard
hold	held	held
lay	laid	laid

Infinitive	Past Tense	Past Participle
lead	led	led
pay	paid	paid
say	said	said
sell	sold	sold
slide	slid	slid
stand	stood	stood
tell	told	told
wake	woke (waked)	waked (woken)
bind	bound	bound
find	found	found
grind	ground	ground
wind	wound	wound
bear	bore	borne
become	became	became
come	came	come
do	did	done
go	went	gone
make	made	made
shine	shone	shone (shined)
beat	beat	beaten
bite	bit	bitten
break	broke	broken
chose	chose	chosen
drive	drove	driven
eat	ate	eaten
fall	fell	fallen
forget	forgot	forgotten
freeze	froze	frozen
get	got	gotten
give	gave	given
hide	hid	hidden
ride	rode	ridden

Infinitive	Past Tense	Past Participle
rise	rose	risen
shake	shook	shaken
speak	spoke	spoken
steal	stole	stolen
take	took	taken
tread	trod	trodden (trod)
weave	wove	woven
write	wrote	written
dig	dug	dug
hang	hung	hung
ring	rang	rung
sing	sang	sung
spring	sprang	sprung
wring	wrung	wrung
drink	drank	drunk
shrink	shrank	shrunk
sink	sank	sunk
stink	stank (stunk)	stunk
swim	swam	swum
be	was	been
begin	began	begun
draw	drew	drawn
lie	lay	lain
run	ran	run
see	saw	seen
spin	spun	spun
tear	tore	torn
wear	wore	worn
win	won	won
blow	blew	blown

Infinitive	Past Tense	Past Participle
fly	flew	flown
grow	grew	grown
know	knew	known
throw	threw	thrown
show	showed	shown (showed)
sow	sowed	sown (sowed)
bring	brought	brought
buy	bought	bought
fight	fought	fought
seek	sought	sought
think	thought	thought
bend	bent	bent
catch	caught	caught
lend	lent	lent
lose	lost	lost
mean	meant	meant
meet	met	met
send	sent	sent
set	set	set
sit	sat	sat
spit	spit (spat)	spit (spat)
teach	taught	taught

REFERENCES

Algeo, John. *Problems in the Origins and Development of the English Language.*
New York: Harcourt Brace Jovanovich Publishers, 1982.

American Heritage Dictionary of the English Language, Fifth Edition. Boston:
Houghton Mifflin Harcourt, 2011. General references see: The Indo-European
Family of Languages, word histories, and word usage notes.

Bryant, Margaret M. "English Language," *Encyclopedia Americana*, 1999,
10:418-426.

English Literature, Baugh, Albert C. and George William McClelland, Eds.
New York: Appleton-Century-Croft, Inc., 1954.

Ethnologue: Languages of the World. Grimes, Barbara F., Ed., 1999.
http://www.sil.org/ethnologue/top100.html

Frost, Robert. *Robert Frost's Poems.* Washington Square Press: New York, 1970.

Google: Merriam Webster's Dictionary, New Words, 2010.

Hughes, Langston. *Selected Poems of Langston Hughes.* New York:
Vintage Books, 1989, 5.

Longfellow, Henry Wadsworth. *The Song of Hiawatha.* Bounty Books:
New York, 1968.

McNeill, William H. "Europe: History." *Encyclopedia Americana,* 1999, 10:689-700.

Modern American Poetry. Untermeyer, Louis, Ed. New York: Harcourt, Brace and Co., 1950.

Origins of Language. "Nature," Nature Publishing Group, 2010. www.nature.com/news/1998/031124/full/new

Poems of American History. Stevenson, Burton Egbert, Ed. Cambridge, Mass: Houghton Mifflin Co., 1950.

Random House Webster's Unabridged Dictionary, Random House Reference, New York, 2001.

Sandburg, Carl. *Harvest Poems 1910-1960*. Harcourt Brace Jovanovich: New York, 1960.

Swiggers, Pierre. "Linguistics: History of Linguistics." *Encyclopedia Americana*, 1999, 17:532K-532P.

The Complete College Reader. Holmes, John and Carroll S. Towle, Eds. Boston: The Riverside Press, 1950.

The Complete Poems of Emily Dickinson. Johnson, Thomas H., Ed. Boston: Little, Brown and Co., 1960.

Thoreau, Henry David. *Walden*. Philadelphia: Running Press, 1990.

Tonkin, Humphrey. "Esperanto." *Encyclopedia Americana*, 1999, 10:583-584.

Victorian Prose and Poetry. Trilling, Lionel and Harold Bloom, Eds. New York:

Oxford University Press, 1973.

References of Quotations

Angelou, Maya. "Quotable Quotes." *Reader's Digest*, June 2001, 73.

Bacon, Francis. "Of Travel." *English Literature*. Ed. Baugh, Albert C. and George William McClelland. New York: Appleton-Century-Crofts, Inc., 1954, 350.

Mill, John Stuart. *Telling Writing.* Upper Montclair, New Jersey: Boynton/Cook Publishers, Inc., 1985, 92.

Newton, Isaac. "Laws of Motion." *The Complete College Reader.* Ed. Holmes John and Carroll S. Towle. Boston: The Riverside Press, 1950, 192.

Sandburg, Carl. "Fog." *Harvest Poems 1910-1960.* San Diego: Harcourt Brace Jovanovich, 1960, 39.

Scott Forsman English Literature and Integrative Studies. Glenview, Ill: Scott Forsman, 1997.

    Browning, Elizabeth Barrett. "Sonnet 43," 539

    Pope, Alexander. "Essay on Criticism," 325.

Sandburg, Carl. "Fog," *Harvest Poems 1910-1960.* San Diego: Harcourt Brace Jovanovich, 1960, 39.

Scott Forsman English Literature and Integrative Studies. Glenview, IL: Scott Forsman, 1997.

Thoreau, Henry David. *Walden.* Philadelphia: Courage Books, 1990, 67.

Walker, Alice. *Her Blue Body Everything We Know.* San Diego: Harcourt Brace Jovanovich, 1991, 228.

Whitman, Walt. *Leaves of Grass.* Doubleday.

Woolf, Virginia. *To the Lighthouse.* San Diego: Harcourt Brace Jovanovich, Publishers, 1955, 301.

Index

PART I:
OUR CHANGING LANGUAGE

Index

PART II:
COMPONENTS, STRUCTURES
AND PRINCIPLES OF ENGLISH

ABOUT THE AUTHOR

Evelyn D. Klein holds a B.S. in Secondary Education from the University of Wisconsin-Milwaukee and an M.S. in the Teaching of English from the University of Wisconsin-River Falls. She taught English, including writing, literature, linguistics and communications as well as German in the public schools in Wisconsin and Minnesota, writing at Century College and the Loft Literary Center, where she also led a poetry group for several years. She is an independent scholar with the Minnesota Independent Scholars Forum and editor of *The Minnesota Scholar.*

A prize-winning poet, her poetry and articles have been published in numerous publications, including the Minneapolis Family Housing Fund's "Home Sweet Home Exhibit," Minnesota Jung Association's *Elements,* and most recently in Ramsey County Library's *This Was 2020.* Her books include *From Here Across the Bridge,* a poetry memoir with woodcuts by Wolfgang Klein, *Once upon a Neighborhood* and *Seasons of Desire,* poetry, essays, and her own illustrations. These three books were both placed in the Minnesota Historical Society's permanent library collection. Her latest book out in 2022, *Fear and Promise, Remembering the Year 2020,* is a chronicle in verse including her own illustrations.